# JAMES JOYCE A LIFE

Gabrielle Carey co-wrote the bestselling *Puberty Blues* while still in her teens, and thereafter published equally acclaimed books of biography, autobiography and memoir. Her book *Moving Among Strangers*, a study of the poet and novelist Randolph Stow, was the joint winner of 2014 Prime Minister's Award for Non-Fiction and shortlisted for the 2015 National Biography Award. In 2020 her *Only Happiness Here: In Search of Elizabeth von Arnim* led to shortlisting for the Hazel Rowley Literary Fellowship. *James Joyce: A Life* reveals her very deep and lifelong interest in Joyce and her fascination for Irish literature.

*By Gabrielle Carey*—

*Puberty Blues*, co-authored with Kathy Lette
(McPhee Gribble, 1979)

*Just Us* (Penguin Books, 1984)

*In My Father's House*
(Pan Macmillan Publishers Australia, 1992)

*The Borrowed Girl* (Picador, 1994)

*The Penguin Book of Death*, co-edited with Rosemary
Sorensen (Penguin Books, 1997)

*So Many Selves* (ABC Books, 2006)

*Waiting Room* (Scribe Publications, 2009)

*Moving among Strangers: Randolph Stow and My Family*
(University of Queensland Press, 2013)

*Falling Out of Love with Ivan Southall*
(Australian Scholarly Publishing, 2018)

*Only Happiness Here: In Search of Elizabeth von Arnim*
(University of Queensland Press, 2020)

# JAMESJOYCEALIFE

*Gabrielle Carey*

Arden

Melbourne & Galway

For the *Finnegans Wake* reading groups of Sydney and Canberra, and especially for Sarah Weate, who made many valuable contributions to this book. Thank you.

First published 2023 by ARDEN
*the international general books' imprint of*
Australian Scholarly Publishing Pty Ltd
7 Lt Lothian St Nth, North Melbourne, Vic 3051, Australia
61+3+93296963 / enquiry@scholarly.info / www.scholarly.info

ISBN 978-1-922952-22-6

*Cover design:* Tohby Riddle, Amelia Walker

# Apologia

I offer this incomplete story of the life of James Joyce as a loving *in memoriam*. It was written with a bower bird approach, the only one that felt natural to me. It is not a scholarly biography and does not provide a complete picture of the man or his work. I humbly request that the reader keep in mind Joyce's forgiving attitude towards mistakes, errors and *misses in prints,* and that we are all, as he says, *human, erring and condonable.*

Of the Gauls, the Greek historian Diodorus Siculus wrote :

*In conversation they use few words and speak in riddles, for the most part hinting at things and leaving a great deal to be understood.*

*Library of History*, 1st century BC

James Joyce, 1926

Photo by Berenice Abbott [Getty's Images]

# — 1 —

James Augustine Aloysius Joyce was born on 2 February 1882 : Candlemas Day. Halfway between the winter solstice and spring equinox, Candlemas Day is a waypoint on the journey out of winter.

> If Candlemas be fair and bright,
> Winter has another flight.
> If Candlemas brings clouds and rain,
> Winter will not come again.
> *Traditional*

Candlemas is also Groundhog Day. James Joyce liked the idea of sharing his day with a groundhog and saw the date as a good omen. Years later he would arrange for his most famous work, *Ulysses*, to be published on his fortieth birthday.

When James was born, the Joyce family was wealthy. James's father, John, had a well-paid job as a rates collector and owned several properties in Cork.

John and May Joyce's first son, born seven months after they married, had died at eight weeks. May would go on to bear another ten children who survived childhood, as well as an uncertain number of miscarriages.

As a boy, the young Joyce seems to have had a sense of his own specialness. His brother Stanislaus, born two years after James, remembers his older brother, accompanied by a maid, tottering down the stairs to the dining room, calling out, 'Here's Me! Here's Me!'

Much later, in *Finnegans Wake*, this refrain would change to *Here Comes Everybody*.

# — 2 —

When Joyce was five, the family moved to a large house in Bray because his father wanted to be closer to the sea and further away from his in-laws. One Martello Terrace, Bray was so close to the sea that it sometimes flooded.

At Bray, the family was joined by a relative who became the children's governess. She taught Joyce to cross himself and pray whenever there was a thunderstorm : 'Jesus of Nazareth, King of the Jews, from a sudden and unprovided for death, deliver us, O Lord.'

Joyce suffered from astraphobia, a terror of thunder and lightning, for the rest of his life. Thunder would also play a role in his books, with *Finnegans Wake* punctuated by ten thunderwords – 100-letter words, incorporating words from other languages and with multiple meanings.

The first thunderword appears on the first page of Joyce's final work :

*bababadalgharaghtakamminarronnkonnbronnton-*
*nerronntuonnthunntrovarrhounawnskawntoohoohoo-*
*rdenenthurnuk!*

While it looks like nonsense, it is actually made up
of the word thunder in various languages (*Gargarahat*
is thunder in Hindi, for example, followed by
*kaminari,* thunder in Japanese.) Most importantly,
it is a statement of one of Joyce's major themes: the
thunderous sound of the fall of man.

Sin was one of Joyce's earliest and most enduring
obsessions. As a small child, he re-enacted the Adam
and Eve story with his younger brother as Adam, and
his sister as Eve. Joyce played the devil, wriggling
around on the floor with a long tail made of a
rolled-up towel.

'He had an instinctive realisation of the fact that
the most important part, dramatically, was that of the
Tempter,' remarked his brother Stanislaus.

At home his nickname was Sunny Jim because of
his happy, easy-going disposition.

— **3** —

At six, being near-sighted, Joyce started wearing
glasses.

At six and a half, he started boarding school at
the Jesuit Clongowes Wood College, one of Ireland's

most exclusive schools. On his arrival, when asked his name, he replied 'half-past six'.

Incidents from his time at Clongowes are given to Stephen Dedalus in *A Portrait of the Artist as a Young Man*, Joyce's semi-autobiographical novel.

In Greek myth, Daedalus is the architect of the Labyrinth of King Minos of Crete and also the father of Icarus, who flew too close to the sun. By his early twenties, Joyce was supremely confident of his future as an architect of literary labyrinths.

At the age of seven, the young Joyce was accused by the college's prefect of studies of deliberately smashing his own glasses. Years later, the scene was recreated in *A Portrait*:

> Stephen stumbled into the middle of the class, blinded by fear and haste.
>
> – Where did you break your glasses? repeated the prefect of studies.
>
> – The cinder-path, sir.
>
> – Hoho! The cinder-path! cried the prefect of studies. I know that trick.

Stephen is given four 'pandies' – corporal punishment administered by a leather strap known as a pandybat. The young Joyce was incensed by the injustice of the incident and complained to the Rector of Clongowes, Father Conmee – one of the many historical characters who appear in Joyce's works.

In real life, Conmee sympathised with the young Joyce, accepted his innocence, and from then on took a keen interest in his bold young student. On perusing the boy's letters home, he observed that they were like grocer's lists. Rather than writing about his time at school, he simply listed items that he wanted his parents to send.

As a mature writer, Joyce continued to have a fondness for lists, some of which go on for pages. A list in *Finnegans Wake* provides a playful self-portrait of the writer's physical features:

> the wrong shoulder higher than the right, an artificial tongue with a natural curl, not a foot to stand on, a handful of thumbs, a blind stomach, a deaf heart, a loose liver, two fifths of two buttocks, a salmonkelt's thinskin ...

Corresponding with a friend many years later, Joyce remembered the priest's comment about his letter-writing and conceded that not much had changed. 'I have a grocer's assistant's mind,' he said.

Joyce was twelve when the students of Clongowes were asked to write an essay on their favourite hero. He chose Odysseus. He liked the fact that the ancient warrior triumphed through cunning and intelligence rather than violence.

As well as an interest in Greek mythology, the young Joyce studied the rituals of the church so devotedly that his Jesuit teachers believed he was headed for the priesthood. Later, Joyce lost his faith in the church, but the influence of Catholicism never left his writing: the idea of *felix culpa* – Latin for 'happy fault' – is central to *Finnegans Wake* and *Ulysses*, and possibly to Joyce's entire philosophy.

*Felix culpa* is a concept in Catholic theology which interprets the faulty or sinful condition of humanity as happy because without it we would not have been given so great a Redeemer. To Joyce, the faulty or sinful condition of humanity is happy because faults, errors, mistakes and misunderstandings are what creates comedy. Both *Finnegans Wake* and *Ulysses*, Joyce insisted, were written with the intention to make people laugh, laughter being the essential relief from life's sufferings.

> Loud, heap miseries upon us yet entwine our arts with laughters low!

The question was, and is always:

> Shall we be *Mr Shallwesigh* or *Mr Shallwelaugh?*

— **4** —

When John Joyce lost his position as a rates collector, the family's annual income plunged from a substantial £500 to a pension of £132. James was removed from Clongowes because his father could no longer afford the fees.

The family's downward spiral continued and over the next decade they moved eight times into ever cheaper and smaller lodgings. Moves that had once necessitated two furniture vans and a float were reduced to a small cartload, as belongings were sold to settle debts.

— **5** —

For two years James was sent to a Christian Brothers school, even though his father referred to the Brothers as 'Paddy Stink and Micky Mud'. It was Joyce's one break with Jesuit education.

Joyce was eleven when a chance encounter between John Joyce and Father Conmee resulted in scholarships being arranged for James and his brother Stanislaus at Belvedere College, another Jesuit institution.

Joyce was a conscientious student. When the family went on picnics, he took his notebooks with lists of French and Latin words and asked his mother to test him.

— **6** —

At the age of fourteen Joyce experienced his first sexual arousal. He was walking home with a young nurse who told him to turn away while she urinated in a field. In a letter, he confessed that the sound of her 'piss' aroused him. 'I jiggled furiously,' he wrote. The experience seems to have resulted in a lifelong erotic interest in women urinating.

In *Ulysses*, Leopold Bloom reflects:

> Chamber music. Could make a pun on that.
> It is a kind of music.

*Chamber Music* is the title of Joyce's first poetry collection.

Urination also plays an important role in the Ithaca chapter when Leopold Bloom and Stephen Dedalus, a kind of spiritual father and son, bond by urinating together in their only moment of longed-for intimacy:

> At Stephen's suggestion, at Bloom's instigation both, first Stephen, then Bloom, in penumbra urinated, their sides contiguous, their organs of micturition reciprocally rendered invisible by manual circumposition, their gazes, first Bloom's, then Stephen's, elevated to the projected luminous and semiluminous shadow.

And in *Finnegans Wake*, a scene of two girls urinating in Phoenix Park is central to the 'crime scene' that implicates the main character, Humphrey Chimpden Earwicker, in sexual misconduct.

Humphrey Chimpden Earwicker, or HCE for short, also stands for Here Comes Everybody. In other words, the entire fallen human race.

James studied hard for the Irish intermediate exams and told his father he wanted two chops if he won an exhibition (the name of a prize given for academic excellence). He won £20. The following year, 1895, he won £20 paid over three years. In 1897, he won £30 paid over two years, and £3 for the best English composition in Ireland. His total exhibition prize money was more than his father's annual income.

John Joyce continued to drink most of his pay packet and take out his frustrations on his family. When James was fifteen, his father tried to strangle his wife, shouting, 'Now, by God, is the time to finish it.' James came to the rescue, knocking down the abuser and pinning him to the floor while his mother escaped to a neighbour's house. May Joyce had only recently recovered from the death of her most recent baby, who had lived for only a few weeks.

Despite his father's fecklessness, James remained extremely fond of him. In *A Portrait*, Stephen Dedalus uses yet another list to inventory his father's attributes:

A medical student, an oarsman, a tenor, an amateur actor, a shouting politician, a small landlord, a small investor, a drinker, a good fellow, a storyteller, somebody's secretary, something in a distillery, a taxgatherer, a bankrupt and at present a praiser of his own past.

# — 8 —

Joyce inherited a number of traits from his father, including his attitude towards money.

While at university, Joyce was paid twelve guineas for a review of Henrik Ibsen's play, *When We Dead Awaken*. He gave his mother £1 to feed the family of nine, and left for London with his father, spending the rest of the money in music halls and theatres.

Ibsen read the review and in a letter to his translator made some complimentary remarks on the young reviewer's reflections. The translator forwarded Ibsen's comments to Joyce, after which Joyce taught himself enough Dano-Norwegian so that he could respond directly to his literary hero. His letter ended:

> As one of the young generation for whom
> you have spoken I give you greeting – not
> humbly, because I am obscure and you in the
> glare, not sadly, because you are an old man
> and I am a young man, not presumptuously
> nor sentimentally – but joyfully, with hope
> and with love, I give you greeting.

Joyce was later to comment to his friend Arthur Power that Ibsen had caused 'the greatest revolution in our time in the most important relationship there is – that between men and women: the revolt of women against the idea that they are the mere instruments of men.'

Another writer who interested Joyce during his university years was the 16th century Italian philosopher Giordano Bruno of Nola. Joyce quoted him in the opening of his self-published and controversial pamphlet titled *The Day of the Rabblement*.

*The Day of the Rabblement* was a broadside against the then fashionable Irish Literary Revival Movement which promoted cultural nationalism and traditional Gaelic culture, a movement that Joyce believed was sentimental, insular and backward-looking, as well as wilfully blind to the harsh reality of Irish life. The Irish Literary Revival Movement was also known as The Celtic Twilight. In *Finnegans Wake*, Joyce calls it the *cultic twalette*.

Joyce's pamphlet accused the Movement of of pandering to 'trolls', the word Ibsen used for the enemies of art.

The quotation Joyce used from Bruno read: 'No man, said the Nolan, can be a lover of the true or the good unless he abhors the multitude; and the artist, though he may employ the crowd, is very careful to isolate himself.'

Giordano Bruno of Nola, who would be a major influence on Joyce, was the first known person to propose that stars are like other suns and have their own planets. His other controversial ideas included the belief that the universe is infinite and that our own planet is not at the centre.

Bruno applied for the Chair of Mathematics at Padua but was turned down in favour of Galileo Galilei.

In 1600, at the age of fifty-two, Bruno was burned at the sake for his heretical claims, which were considered so dangerous that he was gagged even as he burned.

A statue of Bruno now stands in the Campo de Fiori plaza in Rome where he was executed.

While writing *Finnegans Wake*, Joyce utilised Bruno's theory of *coincidentia oppositorum* – the coincidence of opposites. 'His philosophy is a kind of dualism,' Joyce explained in a letter, 'every power in nature must evolve an opposite in order to realise itself and opposition brings reunion.'

This theme – opposition followed by reunion – plays out through Joyce's final work. It's possible Joyce is hinting at the idea that the ultimate reality is not divided into a myriad of manifestations but rather a divine oneness. Although the *Wake* appears to be fragmenting language and sentences and grammar, the intention might well be one of amalgamation and reconciliation. We are, he says:

humble indivisibles in this grand continuum.

# — 9 —

By the time Joyce was in his late teens, he was complaining about the insipid intellectual environment in Dublin, calling it the 'venereal condition of the Irish', and longed to travel to Europe. On finishing university, he decided to study medicine, the degree his father had failed to complete. The plan to enrol in medicine also gave him an excuse to leave the country of his birth because enrolling in the Ecole de Médecine in Paris was cheaper than studying in Dublin. Many years later, he would write of his earlier pretensions to be a doctor: 'I would have been even more disastrous to society at large than I am in my present state had I continued.'

To fund his European plan, Joyce petitioned Lady Gregory, a wealthy and prominent member of the Irish Literary Revival Movement, signing off with the following:

> All things are inconstant except the faith in the soul, which changes all things and fills their inconstancy with light. And though I seem to have been driven out of my country here as a misbeliever I have found no man yet with a faith like mine.

Lady Gregory at first declined and then parted with £5. Joyce left Dublin from Kingstown pier, now Dún Laoghaire, on the evening of 1 December 1902.

*A Portrait of the Artist as a Young Man* ends with Stephen leaving his homeland from the same place and exclaiming:

> Welcome, O life! I go to encounter for the millionth time the reality of experience and to forge in the smithy of my soul the uncreated conscience of my race.

## — **10** —

In 1902 author and critic George Russell wrote to a friend about the young writer he'd recently met in 1902: 'There is a young boy named Joyce who may do something. He is proud as Lucifer.' Sixteen years later in Zurich, the chorus girls at the Stadttheater called Joyce 'Herr Satan', partly because of his goatee beard. In *Finnegans Wake* he would refer to himself as *Mr Tellibly Divilcult*.

At the age of twenty, while en route to Paris, thanks to an introduction from George Russell, Joyce met with W. B. Yeats. They spent an entire day together, and Yeats bought the younger writer breakfast, lunch and dinner.

During the meeting Joyce said to Yeats: 'I am not, as you see, treating you with any deference for after all both you and I will be forgotten.'

After the meeting, Yeats observed: 'Such a colossal self-conceit with such a Lilliputian literary genius I never saw combined in one person.' He would later revise his opinion.

In Paris, Joyce arranged to give English lessons to a champagne dealer for £1 a month. This was his only income.

He constantly requested money from his mother, which she sent even though it meant depriving her other children. On one occasion, she sold a carpet so she could wire money to her brilliant eldest son.

Joyce made a promise to his mother that, once he graduated from medical school, he would buy her a new set of teeth.

However, he had barely begun his studies when he wrote home saying he was finding it difficult to settle down and complained that he felt alone and misunderstood. His mother responded:

> My dear Jim,
> … if as usual I fail to understand what you would wish to explain, believe me it is not from any want of a longing desire to do so and speak the words you want but as you so often said I am stupid and cannot grasp the great thoughts which are yours much as I desire to do so … I only wish I was near you to look after and comfort you but we will be united very soon again thank God home you must come if only for a week.

By this time John Joyce had cashed in part of his

pension to buy a house, leaving the family only 70 pounds a year to live on. He took out a second mortgage to pay for his eldest son's passage home for Christmas. The young writer's self-exile had barely lasted a few weeks.

Back in Dublin, Joyce spent many hours at the National Library. One evening, while waiting at the counter for a book, he fell into conversation with Oliver Gogarty, son of a well-to-do Dublin physician. Gogarty was a medical student with literary pretensions who also had an odd reputation for saving people from drowning. He immediately recognised Joyce's nascent genius.

Gogarty would go on to become famous as an ear, nose and throat specialist, but even more famous as the model for the character Buck Mulligan in *Ulysses*.

# — 11 —

Joyce returned to Paris in early 1903 but spent more time reading Aristotle at the Bibliothéque Nationale than he did attending to his medical studies.

To his friends, he signed off his letters as Stephen Dedalus.

Within weeks he was writing home about being hungry.

Dear Mother,

Your order for 3 shillings and fourpence of Tuesday last was very welcome as I had been without food for 42 hours (forty-two). Today I am twenty hours without food. But these spells of fasting are common with me now ...

Even when she sent money, he complained:

I cannot cash your order today. I do not understand in the least what you write about ... when you spend only three minutes at a letter it cannot be very intelligible ... My next meal therefore will be at 11 a.m. tomorrow (Monday): my last meal was 7pm last (Saturday) night. So I have another fast of 40 hours – No, not a fast, for I have eaten a pennyworth of dry bread.

His mother wrote:

Dear Jim,

Do not despair though for I feel still full of hope for you and this month will tell a great deal _keep all your friends_ and in a suitable time call on Mrs McBride who received you well and whose marriage and love making naturally kept her from looking after more serious business and you will make a big mistake by not keeping as yr Pappie says 'in touch with her' _You cannot get on in your line without friends._

In her letters, his mother only occasionally alluded to her deteriorating health. On returning to his hotel late after a night wandering the streets of Paris, Joyce found a telegram telling him to return home immediately. True to Joyce's sense that most human communication is miscommunication, it had a typographical error: 'Nother dying, come home. Father.'

It was Easter Sunday, and he borrowed the boat fare from his champagne-dealer pupil.

On her deathbed, his mother asked her eldest son to pray for her. He refused.

May Joyce died of liver cancer at the age of forty-four, having carried a total of thirteen pregnancies. Nine of her children survived her.

Joyce later wrote:

> My mother was slowly killed, I think, by my father's ill-treatment, by years of trouble, and by my cynical frankness of conduct. When I looked on her face as she lay in her coffin … I understood that I was looking on the face of a victim and I cursed the system which had made her a victim.

The memory of his dying mother and his refusal to appease her last wishes would haunt Joyce for years to come and eventually resurface in the pages of *Ulysses* where her ghost appears in the opening pages.

Stephen Dedalus – who segues from the protagonist in *A Portrait* to a major character in *Ulysses* – is criticised by his friend Buck Mulligan for his obstinacy:

> You could have knelt down, damn it, Kinch, when your dying mother asked you, Buck Mulligan said. … But to think of your mother begging you with her last breath to kneel down and pray for her. And you refused. There is something sinister in you.

After his wife's death, John Joyce continued his feckless ways, and his name appeared in the section of the *Stubbs Gazette* reserved for blacklisting debtors. The family became further impoverished. They drank tea out of jam jars and ate fried bread with dripping.

Joyce dealt with his grief and his guilt by going out on alcoholic binges. His brother Stanislaus's diary reads: 'Jim home drunk three times in a month and on one occasion sick and dirty on Sunday morning having been out all night.'

While out with his drinking buddy, Oliver Gogarty, Joyce stole a travelling salesman's suitcase full of women's underwear, possibly the beginning of his lifelong fetish for 'drawers'.

In the last chapter of *Ulysses,* Molly Bloom reflects on her husband's obsession with underwear:

> of course hes mad on the subject of drawers thats plain to be seen always skeezing at those brazenfaced things on the bicycles with their skirts blowing up to their navels …

> drawers drawers the whole blessed time till I promised to give him the pair off my doll to carry about in his waistcoat pocket.

# — 12 —

Like his father, Joyce was blessed with a beautiful tenor voice. At the age of 22, with thoughts of being a professional singer, he entered the Feis Ceoil competition, an annual celebration of Irish musical talent. He was awarded a bronze medal, the equivalent to second place. Despite high praise from the judge of the competition, who strongly urged him to pursue musical study, Joyce gave up on the idea of a singing career. When he couldn't pawn his bronze medal, he decided to leave it with his Aunt Josephine. 'I have no use for it,' he wrote. Later, a close colleague would comment: 'Joyce never quite ceased to regret his choice of a writer's instead of a singer's career.'

Not longer after, he posted a short note to a friend in Dublin to say that he was writing what would become his first collection of stories:

> I call the series Dubliners to betray the soul of that hemiplegia or paralysis which many consider a city.

His intention, he would later claim, was to write 'the moral history of my country'.

# — 13 —

On 10 June 1904 James Joyce was walking down

Nassau Street, Dublin, in torn canvas shoes when he met a young Irish woman, Nora Barnacle.

She was twenty; he was twenty-two.

Joyce was five foot nine, very slender, with a golden beard and a towering forehead. At first, Nora thought Joyce was a Swedish sailor with his electric blue eyes, yachting cap and plimsolls. But when he spoke, she knew him at once as just another Dubliner chatting up a country girl.

Nora was auburn-haired and considered by many as strikingly attractive. (Many years later, when sitting for her portrait by painter Tullio Silvestri, the artist described her as the most beautiful woman he had ever seen.) Defiant and spirited, she had run away from her home in Galway after her uncle discovered she had been seeing a Protestant boy. In Dublin, she found work as a chambermaid in Finn's Hotel, just outside the walls of Trinity College.

Joyce arranged to meet her a few days later on 14 June. He waited for hours, but Nora did not appear.

Through an exchange of notes, the rendezvous was rescheduled for 16 June.

The weather in Dublin on 16 June 1922 was unusually warm, fair and bright. That evening James and Nora first walked out together. Of their first outing, Joyce later told Nora: 'You made a man of me.' Apparently it was Nora who took the initiative, unbuttoning her lover's trousers so she could slip in her hand.

That date is now celebrated all over the world as Bloomsday, after Leopold and Molly Bloom, in *Ulysses,* a book set entirely over a single day.

The couple continued to correspond almost every day, sometimes more than once. (In those days there were three deliveries of mail a day.) Within a week Nora was beginning her letters to James with the words 'My Precious Darling' and James was addressing her as 'My dear, dear Nora'.

The idea for Molly Bloom's monologue, which makes up the final chapter of *Ulysses,* and is written in a flowing, unpunctuated form, may have been inspired by one of those early letters from Nora, written just before going to bed:

> Dear Jim I feel so very tired to night I can't say much many thanks for your kind letter which I received unexpectedly this evening I was very busy when the Postman came I ran off to one of the bedroom's to read your letter I was called five times but did not pretend to hear it is now half past eleven and I need not tell you I can hardly keep my eyes open and I am delighted to sleep the night away when I cant be thinking of you so much when I awake in the morning I will think of nothing but you Good night till 7pm to morrow eve.
>
> Nora xxxxxxx

Joyce urged her to write more and soon he was treasuring a total of thirteen letters. He invited her to a concert in Dublin's Antient Concert Rooms in which he was to sing in the same program as the famous Irish tenor John McCormack. Joyce's sweet tenor voice was admired by a review in the *Freeman's Journal*.

The courting of the young couple continued; one evening Joyce playfully stole one of Nora's gloves so he could take it to bed with him.

> it lay beside me all night – unbuttoned – but otherwise conducted itself very properly – like Nora.

Within weeks, his flirtatious light-heartedness was suddenly replaced by a brutal honesty when he felt compelled to tell Nora that he could never offer her the kind of home she no doubt yearned for. When she looked shocked by his confession, he wrote to confirm what he'd said:

> I may have pained you tonight by what I said but surely it is well that you should know my mind on most things? My mind rejects the whole present social order and Christianity – home, the recognised virtues, classes of life and religious doctrines. How could I like the idea of home? My home was simply a middle-class affair ruined by spendthrift habits which I have inherited ... I cannot enter the social order except as a vagabond.

# — 14 —

In September 1904, Oliver Gogarty took out a lease on the Martello Tower in Sandycove, south of Dublin, specifically to give James Joyce, or 'the bard', as he called him, a place to write. He paid £8 for one year. Before the friends could take up residence, Gogarty had to clear out the nesting birds.

A Martello Tower is a type of small round fort, its name deriving from the Italian word *martello*, meaning hammer. The location is now the James Joyce Tower and Museum. Admission is free.

Up until Joyce moved into the Martello Tower in September 1904, he had been couch-surfing, most recently with his Aunt Josephine. But after only a few days his uncle had locked him out due to his drinking habits and late hours.

Gogarty named the Tower the *omphalos* in the hope that it would be the centre for a rebirth of Irish culture and talked with Joyce about wanting to Hellenise Irish literature. Later, Joyce obliged by reimagining Homer's Greek epic, *The Odyssey*, in a single day in Dublin.

The opening chapter of *Ulysses* is set in the Martello Tower. The main room is gloomy and domed. When the heavy door is set ajar, Joyce describes the light and bright air as welcome. The three inhabitants of the Tower are Stephen Dedalus (based on Joyce), Buck Mulligan (based on Gogarty), and a third guest, Haines (based on Samuel Trench, the son of an English major general).

One night, Trench woke from a nightmare about a black panther and fired his gun at his imaginary foe. The shot went into the fireplace beside which Joyce was sleeping, startling the young writer. Gogarty then called out 'Leave him to me' and grabbed the gun which he proceeded to fire at the pots hanging above the fireplace, causing them to fall down on the terrified Joyce. The young writer rose, dressed, and walked the nine miles back to Dublin. He had been in the Tower all of six days.

The incident is recounted in *Ulysses*, with Stephen telling his friend he cannot continue in the Tower while Haines stays there:

> – A woeful lunatic! Mulligan said. Were you in a funk?
>
> – I was, Stephen said with energy and growing fear. Out here in the dark with a man I don't know raving and moaning to himself about shooting a black panther. You saved men from drowning. I'm not a hero, however. If he stays on here I am off.

Gogarty treated the shooting incident as a joke but Joyce, who always retained a fear and loathing of violence, was terrified.

All his life Joyce was a pacifist and disliked any

kind of conflict happening around him, saying, 'I'm a peaceful person.' His form of resistance was irony and comic disdain.

There are only two incidents in *Ulysses* that approximate violent events: (a) the scene in which a biscuit tin is thrown at Leopold Bloom; (b) the scene where Stephen Dedalus is knocked down by two policemen.

Three years later, Samuel Trench, the house guest who caused their estrangement, shot himself in the head, possibly with the very same gun.

The result of the shooting incident was that the friendship between Joyce and Gogarty eventually soured. Later Gogarty told Joyce, 'I don't care a damn what you say of me as long as it is literature.' He is immortalised as Buck Mulligan in the only sentence anyone who has opened *Ulysses* is guaranteed to have read:

> Stately, plump Buck Mulligan came from the stairhead, bearing a bowl of lather on which a mirror and a razor lay crossed.

## — 15 —

Joyce was again longing to leave his native land. His life in an overcrowded, poverty-stricken home amid the oppressive, highly conservative nature of Dublin society offered little hope for the kind of future he envisaged.

Nora also was keen to leave Finn's Hotel where she had been having trouble with the proprietress. She was well aware of the dangers of being a single woman in Dublin, being surrounded by institutions where many a penniless young girl ended up: the National Hospital for Consumption for Ireland, the Asylum for the Female Blind of Ireland, the Retreat for Respectable Protestant Poor, St Patrick's Hospital for Idiots and Lunatics, the Female Orphan House, the Protestant Association for the Education and Support of the Destitute Orphans of Mixed Marriages, as well as the notorious Magdalene laundries for unwed mothers.

In preparation for them to leave Ireland, the young writer wrote to the Berlitz school in London requesting a European post. Next he asked everyone he knew for a loan. When he approached John Yeats, father of WB, Mr Yeats told him he didn't lend to drunkards.

On the day the couple left, Joyce sent short notes around to friends asking for either money, toothbrushes or second-hand clothes. One friend was asked to raid his father's shop.

> As you cannot give me money will you do
> this for me: Make up a parcel of
>> 1 toothbrush and powder
>> 1 nail brush
>> 1 pair of black boots and any coat and
>> vest you have to spare.

These will be very useful. If you are not
here meet me outside Davy Byrne's with
the parcel at 10 past 7. I have absolutely no
boots.

J.A.J.

Davy Byrne's pub is situated at 21 Duke Street,
Dublin and is now famous as the place where Leopold
Bloom stops for lunch on 16 June 1904.

At the bar, Bloom eats a gorgonzola cheese
sandwich with a glass of burgundy, reflecting on his
first kiss with Molly.

Hot I tongued her. She kissed me. I was
kissed. All yielding she tossed my hair.
Kissed, she kissed me.

## — 16 —

Less than four months after their first meeting, Nora
and James ran away together, departing by boat from
the quay known as the North Wall. The scandal that
would ensue among Dubliners, including Joyce's own
family when they heard that he and Nora were living
in sin, was something the young rebel was looking
forward to. Part of his destiny as a writer, he believed,
was to rattle the Irish Catholic conservatism which in
his view paralysed his fellow Dubliners, resulting in
lives of obedient misery.

When John Joyce learned that his son had left for

the Continent with a woman named Barnacle, he quipped that she would never leave him.

The young lovers' destination was Zurich, where Joyce believed a job awaited him at the Berlitz School. They only had enough money to get them as far as Paris. In Paris, Joyce borrowed fifty francs from Dr Joseph Riviére, founder of the Institut Physicothérapique, thanks to an introduction from Lady Gregory.

When they arrived in Zurich there was no work. They were surprised at the cleanliness and order of the city compared with their home town, commonly referred to as dear dirty Dublin -- or *teary turty Taubling* in *Finnegans Wake*. Nora was reprimanded by a policeman for littering.

Joyce wrote to his brother Stanislaus asking if any scandal had erupted in Dublin yet. He added a postscript telling Stanislaus that Nora was no longer a virgin: *Finalement, elle n'est pas encore vierge; elle est touché.*

## — **17** —

On New Year's Eve, 1904, Joyce wrote to his Aunt Josephine saying he was hoping to move on to Italy and enclosed a message for those who had predicted he would abandon his unwed lover.

It was this night three months ago that we

left the North Wall. Strange to say I have not
yet left her on the street, as many wise men
said I would.

# — 18 —

Two months later James and Nora moved again with
the hope of finding a position at the Trieste branch
of the Berlitz School. However there was no vacancy
there either.

They had barely arrived when Joyce managed
to get arrested after intervening in a fight between
three drunken British sailors. As a result, he was
briefly placed in custody and almost deported back to
Ireland. This incident would later provide material for
the mysterious crime at the centre of *Finnegans Wake*.

Next stop was the Berlitz branch in Pola, the naval
port of the Austro-Hungarian empire. He earned £2
a week teaching English and Italian to officers of the
Austrian navy, hoping he could save enough to have
his teeth fixed, which were rotting.

> My mouth is full of decayed teeth and my
> soul of decayed ambitions.

The couple moved into a tiny room where, after
long days of teaching, Joyce wrote while sitting on the
bed.

In March 1905, he was transferred back to the
Berlitz School in Trieste. He and Nora would spend

the next eleven years there.

Joyce's English exercises for his Berlitz students included translation tasks such as:

> 'That lady has nice small breasts.'
>
> 'The tax collector's an imbecile who's always bothering me.'
>
> 'Ireland is a great country. They call it the Emerald Isle. It is now an untilled field. The government sowed it with famine, syphilis, superstition, and alcoholism there. Puritans, Jesuits, and bigots have sprung up.'
>
> 'Proverbially and by nature our peasants walk in their sleep, closely resembling fakirs in their froglike and renunciatory sterility.'

This idea that his fellow countrymen were sleepwalking through their lives would find expression in *Finnegans Wake* many years later when he used the title, which many interpret as having an implied exclamation mark, to exhort all Finnegans (Irishmen) to wake up.

Joyce enjoyed the multicultural aspect of Trieste, which was then the greatest port of the Austro-Hungarian empire. He spent much time chatting with Greek sailors, eventually learning to speak Greek fluently as well as the Triestino dialect. Joyce also spoke Italian, French, German, Spanish and Dutch, as well as Norwegian, Swedish, Danish and

Yiddish. *Finnegans Wake* features over 60 languages.

By this time Joyce was firmly in the habit of living in debt, often requesting advances from his employer, or repaying a loan in the morning only to borrow again in the evening.

When Nora fell pregnant with their first child, the landlady expelled the pair from their lodgings. Throughout her pregnancy Nora felt unwell and blamed the Trieste climate. She had difficulty learning the language, had no friends and cried a lot, presumably homesick.

'I do not know what strange creature she will bring forth after all her tears morose,' Joyce wrote to his brother.

Adding to Nora's unhappiness were Joyce's drinking habits. She never knew what time of the night Joyce would arrive home nor in what state. Often he was so inebriated that he was unable to make his way home and ended up propping himself against a street-corner. Nora's father had also been a heavy drinker and the reason for her parents' separation. She may have felt that she had found herself in exactly the same situation as her mother, only worse because she was unmarried and in a foreign country without family or friends.

In a letter to his aunt, Joyce commented that Nora

does not seem to make much difference

between me and the rest of the men she has known.

Amid the drinking and the teaching and the intense Trieste summer heat ('I hate a damn silly sun that makes men into butter,' he wrote home), he still found time to work on the collection of stories that would become *Dubliners*.

> Many of the frigidities of 'The Boarding House' and 'Counterparts' were written while the sweat streamed down my face,

he wrote to Stanislaus.

> I am uncommonly well pleased with these stories.

Nora gave birth to a boy with the assistance of a doctor who was one of Joyce's private pupils. Two days later the new father wrote to Stanislaus:

> It was not very pleasant for me – the six hours – but it must have been a damn sight worse for Nora.

For two months the newborn remained unnamed. Joyce wrote to his brother saying he thought a child should be allowed to take his father's or mother's name and insisted that the baby would not be baptised. (Paternity is a legal fiction, he would later write in *Ulysses*.)

The child was eventually called Giorgio after

James's much-loved younger brother, George, who had died of typhoid fever at the age of fourteen.

Joyce continued to work on his collection of stories, often writing to relatives for exact information about Dublin life, places and traditions.

> Dear Stannie,
>
> Please send me the information I ask you for as follows:
>
> The Sisters – Can a priest be buried in a habit?
>
> Ivy Day in the Committee Room – Can a municipal election take place in October?
>
> A Painful Case – Are the police at Sydney Parade of the D division?

One preoccupation that never ceased to be fundamental to him was fidelity to fact, wrote Richard Ellmann, Joyce's most famous biographer.

Nora's biographer, Brenda Maddox, agrees:

> Joyce, seeking realism, was always uncomfortable in inventing details for his fiction and preferred to draw from real evidence.

Encouraged by James, in October 1905 Stanislaus set out to join his brother's family in Trieste. After several days' travel in third- and fourth-class train carriages, the twenty-year-old arrived to find that between them the couple had one *centesimo*.

Joyce arranged for Stanislaus to take a position at Berlitz, the entire salary from which he was expected to hand over for household expenses. Stannie also made a loan of a pair of trousers to his brother. The trousers were never returned.

Nora was hoping that sensible, responsible Stanislaus might be a good influence on James. When James went out drinking, it was his brother's job to bring him home. One night, Stanislaus found Joyce in the gutter and asked,

> Do you want to go blind? Do you want to go about with a little dog?

Stanislaus was concerned about his brother's eyesight, which had always been weak, and seemed to worsen with the consumption of alcohol.

During this period, Joyce finished the short story collection that he had started writing the previous year at the age of twenty-two in Dublin and in November 1905, he submitted it to a London publisher, Grant Richards, under the title *Dubliners*.

## − **19** −

In early 1906 Joyce received an offer from Richards. This was accepted and a contract followed: the volume was to be published in that same year and priced at five shillings.

Joyce wrote to his publisher with specific instructions for the printer to follow his punctuation exactly:

> Inverted commas, for instance, to enclose dialogue always seemed to me a great eyesore ...

To Joyce, inverted commas were perverted commas, and his books indicate dialogue with an em-dash.

Two months later, Richards wrote to Joyce saying the printer had refused to print the sample pages he had been requested to produce. He had scrawled on the second proof, 'We cannot print this,' and sent it back. The printer particularly objected to the ironically titled story 'Two Gallants' and insisted on changes to 'Counterparts' as well as an alternative word for 'bloody' in the story 'Grace'. He did not object to 'An Encounter', possibly the most controversial of all the stories, perhaps because he didn't realise that 'the old josser' was masturbating and that Joyce was hinting at paedophilia.

Joyce replied saying that he would change nothing. However, eventually he did concede to some amendments. When Richards requested more, Joyce responded:

> The points on which I have not yielded are the points which rivet the book together [...] I fight to retain them because I believe that in composing my chapter of moral history

in exactly the way I have composed it I have taken the first step towards the spiritual liberation of my country.

The prospect of contributing to spiritually liberating an entire nation did nothing to sway the publisher. Richards wrote with further concerns, to which Joyce replied defensively:

> Your suggestion that those concerned in the publishing of *Dubliners* may be prosecuted for indecency is in my opinion an extraordinary contribution to the discussion [...] I have written nothing whatever indecent in *Dubliners* [...] I seriously believe that you will retard the course of civilisation in Ireland by preventing the Irish people from having one good look at themselves in my nicely polished looking glass.

He was twenty-four years old.

## — **20** —

In July 1906, the couple and their son left Trieste for Rome, where Joyce had organised more secure employment.

In Rome, he took up a position in the Italian correspondence department of Nast-Kolb and Schumacher Bank, where he translated between 200 and 250 letters a day.

He worked from eight in the morning until seven-thirty at night. The seat of his pants had worn so thin that even during the Roman summer, he had to keep his coat on all day. Some customers complained to the management about his appearance.

He wrote to his brother:

> Eglington was sure I would come back begging to Dublin and J.J.B. that I would become a drunkard and Cosgrave that I would become a nymphomaniac. Alas, gentlemen, I have become a bank clerk.

Rome disappointed Joyce and in a letter he described the ancient city as

> a heap of bones and skeletons.

It reminded him, he wrote,

> of a man who lives by exhibiting to travellers his grandmother's corpse.

The English tourists who came to pore over the ruins also irritated him.

Writing repeatedly to Stanislaus to request loans, he explained that

> the real reason the money goes so quickly is that we eat enormously

and then listed – because making lists was one of his favourite pastimes – the components that constituted Nora's usual dinner:

Two slices of roastbeef, 2 polpetti, a tomato
stuffed with rice, part of a salad and half-litre
of wine

To increase his income, Joyce took on private
English students in the evening. He would get home
from the bank at seven forty-five and then give a
lesson between eight and nine.

In a letter to his brother he added a P.P.S.:

I have a new story for *Dubliners* in my head.
It deals with Mr Hunter.

Alfred H. Hunter was a Jewish Dubliner, rumoured
to have an unfaithful wife.

The short story was to be titled *Ulysses*. It was
destined to become much more.

## — 21 —

Seven months after his offer, Richards broke the
*Dubliners* contract and refused to publish. Under
English law at the time printers as well as publishers
were legally responsible for the books they produced
and therefore equally liable for prosecution for
obscenity or libel. One story referred to Queen
Victoria as 'that bloody old bitch'.

Joyce consulted the English consul about taking
legal action. He also wrote to the English Society of
Authors. Neither could provide assistance. 'I cannot

write without offending people,' Joyce wrote in a letter to Richards.

The Joyces' landlady raised the rent, perhaps in the hope of being rid of her tenant with the rowdy, late-night drinking habits.

Joyce wrote to Stanislaus:

> I wish someone was here to talk to me about Dublin.

Possibly homesick, Joyce began to read Irish newspapers, taking a special interest in court cases. A divorce case involving an eighty-five-year-old Jewish jeweller who had had an affair with his eighty-year-old maid caught his attention. In *Ulysses*, the Jewish Bloom enjoys a flirtation, possibly an affair, with the housemaid.

He wrote to his brother:

> I thought of beginning my story *Ulysses*
> but I have too many cares at present. To
> economise we have given up drinking wine
> at lunch. But even then we would not
> live on Lire 25 a week [...] You can see
> how impossible it is for me to write or do
> anything in such circumstances.

One of his cares was the fact that the landlady had finally given the family notice to vacate.

While Joyce searched for alternative accommodation, the couple was so impoverished they could only rent a room for one night at a time. Each night's English lesson would secure the next night's accommodation.

Nora's daily routine was to vacate a rented room by midday and then hang about in a café or a park with young Giorgio until she had the money to get lodgings.

The couple slept head to toe – just as Molly and Leopold do in *Ulysses* – in an attempt to avoid another pregnancy. Nevertheless, Nora fell pregnant again.

Joyce's teeth continued to rot.

And the idea for his next book continued to form.

The idea was to write a story about one day in the life of an ordinary Dubliner, a story that would tell the truth of reality as he had known it in Ireland rather than the myths and legends and fairy stories so popular with the Celtic Twilighters of the Irish Literary Revival Movement.

In his poetry collection *Pomes Penyeach* Joyce rebuffs the Irish Revivalists' fondness for romanticising:

> That they may dream their dreamy dreams
>
> I carry off their filthy streams.

He wrote to Stanislaus about the hypocrisy of Irish society:

> I am nauseated by their lying drivel about

> pure men and pure women and spiritual love
> and love for ever: blatant lying in the face of
> truth.

And his frustration about Rome:

> I think we shall have to go to a hotel. I
> cannot get a room. They want 70 or 80
> Lire a month for rooms, don't want couples
> or children, don't want to give the use of a
> kitchen. I went to agents put an advt in the
> paper, walked miles: no use ... If anyone
> asks ... tell them I think it is the stupidest old
> whore of a town ever I was in.

## − 22 −

Joyce's final disillusionment with Rome came when
he was mugged after a night's drinking and the entire
contents of his wallet – a month's wages from his bank
job – were stolen. A telegram was sent to Stanislaus in
Trieste:

ARRIVING TOMORROW AT EIGHT PENNILESS

Initially, the director of the Scuola Berlitz was not
keen to re-employ Joyce but eventually offered him six
hours of teaching. His old pupils were happy to have
him back.

That summer, Joyce fell ill with rheumatic fever as
a result of one of his drunken sojourns in the gutter.
He spent a few weeks in the Ospedale Civico di Trieste

and then another couple of months convalescing at home. During this period, he began work on 'The Dead', which was intended to be a novel but would become the final and crowning story of *Dubliners*. It is now considered one of the greatest short stories ever written.

On 26 July 1907, Nora gave birth to their second child, a daughter, in the same hospital where Joyce was recuperating. Later she would recount that the baby had been born 'almost in the street'. Mother and child were placed in the pauper's ward and then days later they returned to their flat, while the father remained in hospital.

Fearing blindness, Joyce named the child Lucia Anna after the patron saint of eyes. He was possibly also thinking of Saint Lucia's role as illuminator and messenger in Dante's *Inferno*. The baby was registered erroneously as Anna Lucia. Much later, Joyce would choose the name Anna Livia for the main female character in *Finnegans Wake*.

Stanislaus borrowed from his boss at the Berlitz school to pay for the confinements of both Nora and James. On leaving the pauper's ward of the hospital, Nora was given twenty crowns in charity. Whereas she had easily and happily breastfed her first-born, she did not breastfeed her daughter, presumably because her life was in turmoil. Joyce was still in hospital, two-year-old Georgio was demanding, Stanislaus in debt and taciturn, and the Triestine summer oppressive.

Notwithstanding his added family responsibilities, when Joyce finally recovered he resigned from the Berlitz School with a plan to devote himself entirely to private teaching. However, his habit of staying out late and getting drunk, sometimes with students, was also affecting his reputation. Once, on arriving at a student's home to give a private language lesson, Joyce was so intoxicated that he passed out on the floor.

## — 23 —

As Joyce was going out one evening in 1908, leaving Nora with two young children, she cried out:

> Yes, go now and get drunk. That's all you're good for [...] faith I tell you I'll have the children baptised tomorrow.

Nora did not carry out her threat and the children continued to be listed on official forms as *senza confessione*.

Realising that drinking exacerbated his eye trouble, Joyce announced that he was giving up alcohol. His attempt at abstinence was short-lived. Another attack of iritis, inflammation of the iris, was so severe that leeches were applied, frightening him enough to cause him to give up drinking again, this time for several months.

Joyce's problems with his eyes would be lifelong; he endured more than a dozen operations to try to halt the gradual deterioration of his eyesight. None was under general anaesthetic. He remained awake throughout for each of them.

Nora fell pregnant again, but in August 1908 she suffered a miscarriage. Joyce scrutinised the foetus with sorrow and regret. This experience would also be absorbed into *Ulysses*. While wandering around Dublin, Bloom reflects on the loss of his eleven-day-old son Rudy, a loss that results in the marriage of Leopold and Molly becoming almost sexless, and presumably the reason for Molly's affair with Blazes Boylan.

# − 24 −

Joyce took his son Giorgio on a visit to Dublin for the summer of 1909. Back in his hometown, the self-exile was cut dead by several acquaintances due to the scandal of his living in sin with Nora.

While in Dublin, Joyce wrote to Nora in a panic after hearing some gossip. He had been told that while they were courting in 1904 she had also been seeing another man. Intensely jealous by nature, he immediately wrote to Nora:

At the time I used to meet you at the corner
of Merrion Square and walk out with you and
feel your hand touch me in the dark and hear
your voice [...] you kept an appointment with
a friend of mine outside the Museum, you went
with him along the same streets, down the canal
[...] You stood with him: he put his arm round
you and you lifted your face and kissed him.
What else did you do together? And the next
night you met me!

Write to me, Nora, for the sake of my dead love.

Two weeks later he wrote again to Nora after being
reassured by a friend that the rumour he'd heard was
all a 'blasted lie'.

Guide me, my saint my angel [...] <u>Everything</u>
that is noble and exalted and deep and true and
moving in what I write comes, I believe, from
you.

Joyce then travelled to Galway to meet Nora's
mother for the first time, where she sang him 'The
Lass of Aughrim', one of her daughter's favourite
songs.

The song tells the story of a young woman who has
been seduced by a lord. She is knocking at his castle
door on a cold and rainy night with her infant at her
breast but he won't let her in. It ends:

My babe lies cold within my arms
but none will let me in.

Afterwards Joyce wrote to Nora to say it had

> been worth coming to Ireland to have got the
> air from your poor kind mother.

He would later immortalise the song by using it to create the crucial turning point in 'The Dead', which ultimately leads to one of the most beautiful literary passages ever written. Like all great artists, through the creative process, he metamorphosed grief and tragedy into beauty:

> His soul had approached that region where dwell the vast hosts of the dead. He was conscious of, but could not apprehend, their wayward and flickering existence. His own identity was fading out into a grey impalpable world: the solid world itself which these dead had one time reared and lived in was dissolving and dwindling.

> A few light taps upon the pane made him turn to the window. It had begun to snow again. He watched sleepily the flakes, silver and dark, falling obliquely against the lamplight. … Yes, the newspapers were right: snow was general all over Ireland. It was falling on every part of the dark central plain, on the treeless hills, falling softly upon the Bog of Allen and, farther westward, softly falling into the dark mutinous Shannon waves. It was falling too, upon every part of the lonely churchyard on the hill where Michael Furey lay buried. It lay thickly drifted on the crooked crosses and

headstones, on the spears of the little gate,
on the barren thorns. His soul swooned as
he heard the snow falling faintly through the
universe and faintly falling, like the descent of
their last end, upon all the living and the dead.

This famous ending was in great part inspired by
Nora, just as the famous end of *Ulysses* is. Michael
Furey was the name Joyce gave to the real-life Michael
Bodkin, the teenaged boy who was so besotted with
Nora that he spent an entire snowy winter's night
outside her window, a devotion which led to his
premature death.

On returning to Dublin from Galway, Joyce came
face to face with the reality of his impoverished
family. Five of his sisters were still living with their
father and Joyce decided to bring one, Eva, back to
Trieste. This was probably partly out of pity and and
partly out self-interest. Eva could be a companion for
Nora and also help out with the children.

On the eve of his departure from Ireland, Joyce
wrote to Nora:

> I loathe Ireland and the Irish. Perhaps they
> read my hatred of them in my eyes. I see
> nothing on every side of me but the image of
> the adulterous priest and his servants …

Upon their reunion in Trieste, James gave Nora
a necklace inscribed: 'Love is unhappy when love is
away'. Stanislaus, who had been left to support Nora
and Lucia, mumbled that love's brother was too.

# — 25 —

In Trieste, Joyce's sister enjoyed the novelty of her new surroundings, in particular the cinemas, and commented how odd it was that Trieste had a number of cinemas, whereas Dublin had none.

This remark, according to Joyce's biographer Ellmann, 'set James off like a fuse'. He approached a local group of businessmen saying, 'I know a city of 500,000 inhabitants where there is not a single cinema.' The group was persuaded of the potential for profit and agreed to pay for Joyce to return to Dublin to act as their agent.

Bankrolled by wealthy Triestine investors, Joyce returned to Dublin in August 1909 and booked to stay at Finn's Hotel, keen to see the room that Nora had inhabited. Joyce was genuinely excited about the artistic potential of film and worked hard to establish Dublin's first permanent cinema, The Volta, which opened in December of that year.

The other objective of his trip was to find a new publisher for *Dubliners*. While there, Joyce signed a contract with George Roberts, managing director of Maunsel & Co., who had already published other controversial works such as Synge's *Playboy of the Western World*. When Roberts wasn't publishing, he was an actor in the Abbey Theatre and a travelling salesman of women's undergarments. It is not known whether the two men bonded over this common interest.

Joyce missed Nora intensely and it was during this period that he wrote the now famous 'dirty letters' musing on:

> the idea of a shy beautiful young girl like Nora pulling up her clothes behind and revealing her sweet white girlish drawers in order to excite the dirty fellow she is so fond of; and then letting him stick his dirty red lumpy pole in through the split of her drawers and up up up in the darling little hole between her plump fresh buttocks.

And declaring he:

> wanted to be like a hog riding a sow, glorying in the open shame of your upturned dress and white girlish drawers.

Another letter was signed off:

> Goodnight, my little farting Nora, my dirty little fuckbird! There is one lovely word, darling, you have underlined to make me pull myself off better. Write more about that and yourself, sweetly, dirtier, dirtier.

The above extracts form part of a series of correspondence from which all of Nora's letters are missing. It has been surmised by some that her epistles were equally as dirty, and were written partly out of desire and partly with the intention of keeping Joyce away from the Dublin brothels.

In 2004, one of the dirty letters sold at Sotheby's to a mystery buyer for £240,000. Other Joyce memorabilia at the same auction were bought by popular Irish Riverdance entrepreneur Michael Flatley, for what was reported as 'a small fortune'. These items included Joyce's gold spectacles, the bronze medal he won at the 1904 singing competition, and his cigarette case.

## — **26** —

Joyce soon tired of the Volta enterprise and returned to Trieste in January 1910, this time with his sister Eileen. The cinema failed to be profitable and was sold the following year.

As Joyce's new publisher George Roberts became increasingly nervous about releasing a book that would inevitably provoke controversy, he requested further amendments to the text, including the removal of all references to the king in the story 'Ivy Day'. In response, Joyce decided to write to the king himself, King George V, enclosing a printed proof of the story with the disputed passage marked. He asked King George to let him know 'whether in his view the passage should be withheld from publication as being offensive to the memory of his father.' A reply from the king's secretary informed Joyce that it was 'inconsistent with rule for His Majesty to express his opinion in such cases.'

Next Roberts insisted Joyce change every proper name because he had been advised by solicitors that using actual names of real pubs could be libellous. Finally, the printer decided he wanted nothing to do with such a book and destroyed the sheets that he had printed.

## — 27 —

In 1911, after eight years of being away, Nora travelled back to Ireland with Lucia who was aged four. Together they went to see Ireland's most famous illuminated manuscript, the *Book of Kells,* on display in the Trinity College library.

*The Book of Kells* is a Latin transcription of the Four Gospels from the Middle Ages. It was produced in a monastery founded by St Columba, and for centuries housed in the abbey of Kells, County Meath.

Of his own copy, Joyce said:

> In all the places I have been to, Rome, Zurich, Trieste, I have taken it about with me, and have pored over its workmanship for hours. It is the most purely Irish thing we have.

Nora had travelled ahead without Joyce in the hope that she could convince her uncle to pay for the passages of James and Giorgio. The plan did not come to fruition and again Joyce had to borrow money so he could follow with Giorgio five days later.

In Dublin he met with George Roberts to discuss *Dubliners*. The publisher, a stern Ulsterman, was still adamant that offensive passages would need to be removed before he could commit. Joyce then travelled on to Galway where Nora was visiting her family. A few weeks later he was back in Dublin to continue negotiations with Roberts. As a way of allaying the publisher's fears of libel, Joyce had sought out and paid for a legal opinion. The opinion, however, said just the opposite, remarking on Dublin's Vigilance Committee whose business it was to sniff out and suppress writings of immoral tendencies. The story 'The Encounter' was singled out by the lawyer as particularly troublesome and he advised replacing it with a nice clean story instead.

Joyce wrote to Nora, who was still in Galway:

> I am one of the writers of this generation
> who are perhaps creating at last a conscience
> in the soul of this wretched race.

Roberts, however, was not interested in the creation of a national conscience.

Next Joyce offered to indemnify his publisher at a cost of sixty pounds. But by then it was clear that Roberts had no intention of or interest in publishing

*Dubliners*. The publishing deal fell through and Joyce began his journey back to Trieste, vowing never to return to Dublin. To vent his frustration, while waiting on a train station, he wrote a poem on the back of his publishing contract, which began:

> Ladies and gents, you are here assembled
> To hear why earth and heaven trembled
> Because of the black and sinister arts
> Of an Irish writer in foreign parts.

On his way home, he stopped in London to offer *Dubliners* to Mills and Boon. It was rejected within a week.

Joyce wrote to Yeats:

> I suppose you have heard of the fate of my book *Dubliners*. Roberts refused to publish it and finally agreed to sell me the first edition for £30 so that I might publish it myself. Then the printer refused to hand over the 1000 copies which he had printed either to me or to anyone else and actually broke up the type and burned the whole first edition.

## — 28 —

In 1913, Yeats introduced Joyce to Ezra Pound, who then wrote to Joyce offering his help. Pound showed the manuscript of *A Portrait of the Artist as a Young Man* to Dora Marsden, editor of the avant-garde journal, *The Egoist*.

*The Egoist* had begun under the title *The Freewoman: A Weekly Feminist Review*, then became *The New Freewoman* and then, under the editorship of Ezra Pound, became *The Egoist: An Individualist Review*.

Buoyed by the enthusiasm with which *The Egoist* agreed to publish *A Portrait*, Joyce wrote to Grant Richards, the publisher who had originally contracted *Dubliners* in 1906, asking him to reconsider. Richards agreed to re-contract, suggesting Joyce write a preface in the form of an apology. He refused. By then, Joyce had already written his own preface about

> the deliberate conspiracy of certain forces in Ireland to silence me.

*The Egoist* published the first instalment of *A Portrait of the Artist as a Young Man* on Joyce's thirty-second birthday in 1914.

In June of that year the editorship of *The Egoist* was taken over by Harriet Shaw Weaver. Weaver was an Englishwoman from a wealthy Protestant background, a feminist and a freethinker with a strong social conscience. She had previously spent some years devoted to the Whitechapel Committee of the Society for Organising Charitable Relief and Repressing Mendicity. In many ways the moral opposite to Joyce, she was to become his most important supporter

– among his many female supporters – with the exception of Nora.

On hearing the difficulties Joyce was encountering in his efforts to find a publisher for *A Portrait,* Weaver offered to bring out the book herself, with the assistance of her 'staff', which consisted at the time of one person.

Joyce wrote back, thanking her for the proposal and adding:

> I am writing a book Ulysses and want the other published and out of the way once and for all: and correspondence about publishing is too tiresome for my (very lazy) temperament.

Attempts by Weaver to publish *A Portrait* suffered the same fate as *Dubliners*. Seven printers turned it down with one responding:

> We return the manuscript which you left with us and beg to say that we could not for one moment entertain any idea of publishing such a production.

In the meantime, an American publisher by the name of Ben Huebsch agreed to publish *Portrait* and Weaver's solution to her printer problem was to buy enough sheets from Huebsch to publish 750 copies in England. Joyce wrote:

> But for the enterprise of Miss Weaver, editor of *The Egoist*, in accepting *A Portrait of the Artist*

after it had been refused by all publishers, my novel would still be unpublished.

In June of that year, after protracted negotiations with Richards, *Dubliners* was finally published in an edition of 1250 copies – nine years after it had been written. The cover price was three shillings and sixpence.

Although Joyce had told his publisher that he wanted his fellow Dubliners to be able to see themselves in his 'nicely polished looking-glass', many Dubliners didn't like what they saw. Some considered the stories anti-Irish. The *Irish Book Lover* 'would have preferred that the author had directed his undoubted talents in other and pleasanter directions', and the *Times* ran a review under the headline 'Studies in the Dismal'. Notwithstanding Grant Richards' fears of legal threats, *Dubliners* did not provoke any libel suits.

A year after publication, 379 copies of Joyce's story collection had been sold, 120 of which had been bought by the author. After three years, Joyce had earned exactly two-and-a-half shillings in royalties.

In 2019, a signed first edition of *Dubliners* was sold by Sotheby's for £105,000.

## – 29 –

In 1915, Italy declared war on the Austrian Empire and Trieste became an occupied zone. Joyce and Nora decided to leave the city they had known for ten years. This meant abandoning the income he had derived from teaching in a commercial high school and giving private language lessons.

While the family headed for Zurich, Stanislaus stayed on. The Austrians would later intern him for the remainder of the war because of his vocal support for Italy.

The trip through the Austrian war zone took Joyce, Nora and the children three days. Giorgio was ten, Lucia eight.

In Zurich, they inhabited a series of apartments, supported by grants obtained thanks to W. B. Yeats, who had petitioned various bodies on behalf of the younger impoverished writer. Joyce received £75 from the Royal Literary Fund, £52 from the Society of Authors and £100 from the British Government Civil List. In England grudging respect was growing for Joyce's literary accomplishment while Ireland was still rejecting and criticising his work.

Over the next four years, Joyce and his family would live at seven different addresses while he finished his first novel, his only play, *Exiles*, and nearly half of *Ulysses*.

## — 30 —

*A Portrait of the Artist as a Young Man* was published in New York in 1916. In it, Joyce describes a girl he saw when he was an adolescent, at a time when he was still deeply religious. The young woman was wading in the Irish sea with her skirts tucked up:

> A girl stood before him in midstream, alone and still, gazing out to sea. She seemed like one whom magic had changed into the likeness of a strange and beautiful seabird.

Nora's name Barnacle is derived from the barnacle goose, a large seabird that breeds in the Arctic and visits Irish estuaries during the winter.

> Long, long she suffered his gaze and then quietly withdrew her eyes from his and bent them towards the stream, gently stirring the water with her foot hither and thither …

> Heavenly God! cried Stephen's soul, in an outburst of profane joy.

> Her image had passed into his soul forever.

It was this moment that convinced the young Joyce that the body was integral to a spiritual life, and that his true spiritual path was aesthetic rather than religious. According to Richard Ellmann it was from this point that:

> he started once and for all on his lifelong conviction that literature was the affirmation of the human spirit.

## — 31 —

While writing *Ulysses,* Joyce regularly worked on

the manuscript for ten hours a day. As he wrote, he surrounded himself with rhyming dictionaries, maps, street directories and *Gilbert's History of Dublin.* With him also were multiple Dublin newspapers from 16 June 1904. Joyce wrote to a friend:

> I'm quite content to go down to posterity as a scissors and paste man.

He often called on his Irish friends and relatives for concrete information, such as the type of pianola in a particular Dublin brothel. To his aunt Josephine he wrote:

> Another thing I wanted to know is whether there are trees (and of what kind) behind the Star of the Sea church in Sandymount visible from the shore.

Joyce commented that on the basis of his book it would be possible to reconstruct Dublin a thousand years later just as it was at the beginning of the twentieth century.

Sandymount Beach is the location in *Ulysses* for the scene that arguably provoked more controversy and accusations of obscenity than any other in the book.

Apart from writing, Joyce spent time in Zurich drinking regularly with a small group of international refugees who called themselves the *Club des Étrangers.*

His eye complaints increased, with attacks of

glaucoma, a disease of the retina that can lead to blindness. Joyce took to wearing an eye patch to rest his weaker eye. Later, he described himself as 'an international eyesore'.

Joyce appeared in *Who's Who 1916*. That same year *Dubliners* found an American publisher but six months after publication only seven copies had sold.

In August 1916, on receiving £100 from the British Civil List, Joyce wrote to thank the Prime Minister Asquith's secretary, Edward Marsh

> for being so kind as to bring my books to the notice of the prime minister ... Allow me to assure you that I am deeply grateful to you for having used your influence so generously and so effectively on my behalf and to thank you also for the favourable opinion which you have expressed of my meagre writings.

Joyce considered 1916 a lucky year for him and insisted that his American publisher, Ben Huebsch, release *A Portrait* in the United States before the year was out. The publication date of the very first edition in book form was 29 December.

## – 32 –

On a February afternoon in 1917, while sitting in a darkened room of his Zurich apartment recuperating from eye trouble, Joyce received a registered letter:

Dear Sir,

We are instructed to write to you on behalf of an admirer of your writing, who desires to be anonymous, to say that we are to forward you a cheque for £50 on the 1st May, August, November and February next, making a total of £200, which we hope you will accept without any enquiry as to the source of the gift.

Yours faithfully,

Slack Monro Saw & Co.

Joyce wrote to the lawyers, asking that his message of thanks be passed on.

Dear Sir (or Madam),

... First of all I will ask you to forgive my delay in answering. Since 4 February I have been laid up with a painful and dangerous illness of the eyes ... I am deeply touched by your generosity. I scarcely know what to say. It has given me the greatest encouragement and, coming at such a time as the present, relieves my mind of many worries. Allow me to express my sincere gratitude both for the munificence of your gift, and for the delicacy of its giving. I hope that the future may justify in some measure an act so noble and considerate.

*A Portrait of the Artist as a Young Man* was published in London in February 1917, despite seven printers refusing to set the type and demanding deletions. Ezra Pound suggested that blank spaces be left by the printers and that the deleted passages be pasted in at the publishing offices. 'I can paste them in myself,' he said. The front cover states the publisher as The Egoist Ltd., Oakley House, Bloomsbury St, London. The price was 6 shillings.

That summer the writer's eye complaints increased and an iridectomy was performed on Joyce's right eye which led to his collapse for three days.

Doctors advised him to leave Zurich and spend some time in Locarno and in October the family departed.

While holidaying in Locarno, Joyce became infatuated with a German doctor named Gertrude Kaempffer. He wrote her letters in which he professed his love, spoke of his hope that she reciprocated, and that she could decide how intimate their relationship should be. Gertrude tore up the letters and did not reply.

In Locarno Joyce completed the three initial episodes of *Ulysses*. Gertrude Kaempffer would partly inspire the naming of 'Gerty', the young woman on Sandymount Beach, the sight of whom arouses Leopold Bloom to masturbate.

In January 1918, the Joyce family travelled back to Zurich and took a flat at 38 Universitätstrasse, their sixth address in that city, where he continued work on *Ulysses*.

By this time, thanks to the publication of *A Portrait,* Joyce's reputation as a new force in modern literature had been established.

At a Zurich dinner party Joyce met the English artist Frank Budgen, who was to become one of his closest friends. Budgen described their first meeting thus:

> I saw a tall slender man come into the garden through the restaurant. Swinging a thin cane, he walked deliberately down the steps to the gravelled garden path. He was a dark mass against the orange light of the restaurant glass door, but he carried his head with the chin up-lifted so that his face collected cool light from the sky. His walk as he came slowly across to us suggested that of a wading heron.

One day, Budgen asked how *Ulysses* was progressing:

> 'I have been working hard on it all day,' Joyce answered.
>
> 'Does that mean that you have written a great deal?' asked Budgen.
>
> 'Two sentences,' said Joyce.
>
> 'You have been seeking the *mot juste?*'
>
> 'No,' said Joyce. 'I have the words already. What I am seeking is the perfect order of words in the sentence.'

The sentence for which he was seeking perfect order was:

> Perfume of embraces all him assailed.
> With hungered flesh obscurely, he mutely
> craved to adore.

Joyce continued to drink heavily and Nora became so infuriated that when he returned from a night out, she told him she had ripped up his manuscript. Joyce instantly sobered up and remained so until he discovered she was bluffing. Fed up, she demanded that he switch from absinthe to wine. From then on, Fendant de Sion du Valais, a Swiss wine, became Joyce's favourite beverage. He called it the 'Archduchess most excellent piss', or Archduchess for short. It is a white wine of yellow hue with a sweet edge.

## — 33 —

In 1919 American-born Sylvia Beach sent a telegram to her mother:

> OPENING BOOKSHOP IN PARIS STOP
> PLEASE SEND MONEY

In November of that year Beach opened her shop, which was also a lending library, under the name of Shakespeare and Company at 8 rue Dupuytren.

Of her first meeting with Joyce, Beach wrote:

His eyes, a deep blue, with the light of genius in them, were extremely beautiful ... Joyce's manner was so extremely simple that, overcome though I was in the presence of the greatest writer of my time, I somehow felt at ease with him.

From then on Joyce became an almost daily visitor to the Shakespeare and Company bookshop. Beach was to become another one of Joyce's crucial female supporters, a constant source of loans, both of books and money, and eventually, his publisher.

# — 34 —

Throughout 1919, five instalments from *Ulysses* appeared in *The Egoist*, which was still under Harriet Shaw Weaver's editorship. It caused complaints from readers that the periodical had become unsuitable for the kind of reading matter a decent family left in the living room. Some cancelled their subscriptions.

When Weaver expressed some misgivings about the *Sirens* episode, Joyce responded:

I confess it is an extremely tiresome book but it is the only book which I am able to write at present.

In July 1919, at the end of a business letter to Joyce, Weaver confessed:

Perhaps I had better add that it was I who

sent the message through Messrs Monro, Saw & Co.

And thus the secret benefactor was revealed.

Weaver's vast wealth had been inherited from her mother. It has been speculated that she was conscience-stricken about the idea of living from the profits of usury, believing that her money was hers only in trust and that by giving it to James Joyce, she found a way to relieve her scruples. But there may have been other reasons. According to Weaver's goddaughter, 'Harriet could not be naughty. She needed James Joyce to be naughty for her.' Whatever her motives, Weaver became something of a patron saint, consistently rescuing the writer from financial ruin. Joyce's daughter, Lucia, called her 'Saint Harriet'.

Weaver, who described herself as 'hopelessly English, unadulterated Saxon', would support Joyce for the rest of his life, and even in death, as she would pay the cost of his funeral. He would become almost as dependent on Weaver as he was on Nora.

## — 35 —

Like his father and grandfather, Joyce's son Giorgio was gifted with a beautiful singing voice and was just beginning to take his musical studies seriously when he and Lucia were abruptly taken out of school in Zurich in October 1919 so the family could return to Trieste.

# — 36 —

In late 1919 Weaver wrote to Joyce:

> You are very good for the soul, I think
> medicinal, you are so unflattering to our
> human nature: so, though you are neither
> priest nor doctor of medicine, I think you
> have something of both.*

Joyce responded to Weaver's letter thus:

> It is very consoling to me that you consider
> me a writer because every time I sit down with
> a pen in my hand I have to persuade myself
> (and others) of the fact.

---

* *That Joyce's work is potentially medicinal is taken quite
seriously by numerous Joyceans. Personally speaking, I have
long considered* Finnegans Wake *a highly effective anti-de-
pressant. And it may indeed have other therapeutic applications.
In 2022, a Tiktok video from @ocdbrain had 175,000 likes.
Over the image of a young girl, the message read:*

> has anyone read finnegans wake? my therapist
> gave it to me to help w my intrusive/obsessive/
> racing thoughts. I just started reading ... it makes
> my mind so clear I've NEVER experienced
> silence & finally know what it feels like. 10/10
> recommend. seriously.

# — 37 —

Work continued on *Ulysses* and in an undated letter
from Trieste Joyce wrote again to his aunt for essential
Dublin details:

> I also want all the information you can
> give, tittletattle, facts etc about Hollis Street
> maternity hospital. Two chapters of my book
> remain unfinished till I have these.

In the summer of 1920, the Joyce family moved to
Paris. They intended to stay a week before going on to
London; they stayed for twenty years. In Paris, Joyce
wrote the last four chapters of *Ulysses* and most of
*Finnegans Wake.*

# — 38 —

Between 1918 and 1920, at the urging of Ezra Pound,
parts of *Ulysses* were published in instalments in the
*Little Review*, an American literary magazine edited
by Margaret Anderson and Jane Heap in Chicago.

On reading the opening of the Proteus episode,
Anderson said:

> This is the most beautiful thing we'll ever
> have.

> *Ulysses* – Part I, Chapter 3

> Ineluctable modality of the visible: at least
> that if no more, thought through my eyes.

Signatures of all things I am here to read,
seaspawn and seawrack, the nearing tide,
that rusty boot. Snotgreen, bluesilver, rust:
coloured signs. Limits of the diaphane ... Shut
your eyes and see.

## — 39 —

In October 1920, the New York Society for the
Suppression of Vice instigated obscenity charges
against the editors of the *Little Review*. They were
particularly offended by the Nausicaa episode,
claiming it was pornographic.

The *People of the State of New York v. Margaret
Anderson and Jane Heap* was heard before three
judges. The scene on Sandymount beach which
depicted Bloom masturbating over the glimpse of
a young girl's underpants was deemed obscene.
Anderson and Heap were found guilty of violating
the New York state law against obscenity, and were
publicly declared to be 'a danger to the minds of
young girls'. They were ordered to spend ten days
in prison or pay a fine of $100, an amount neither
of them had. A wealthy woman in the courtroom
unknown to the defendants offered to pay it on their
behalf. A rumour circulated that the seized copies of
the *Little Review* had been sent to the Salvation Army,
so that fallen women in reform programs could tear
them apart like human shredders. The magazine was

never published again, and Anderson and Heap were left penniless.

Joyce was deeply depressed by the news. It meant that *Ulysses* would not have an American publisher and it would also be vulnerable to pirating. Soon after, he wandered into Shakespeare and Company bookshop where Sylvia and her partner Adrienne Monnier had fondly nicknamed him 'Melancholy Jesus'.

> – My book will never come out now, Joyce complained.

> – Would you let Shakespeare and Company have the honour of bringing out *Ulysses?* Sylvia asked.

Afterwards Sylvia wrote to her sister:

> *Ulysses* is going to make my place famous – Already the publicity is beginning and swarms of people visit the shop ... and if all goes well I hope to make money out of it, not only for Joyce but for me.

Sylvia Beach needed to raise money to publish *Ulysses* so she put out a prospectus and sold subscriptions, a type of pre-order. Subscriptions poured in from people as varied as Ernest Hemingway, Andre Gide, Winston Churchill, Wallace Stevens and Havelock Ellis.

Joyce worked furiously to finish *Ulysses*, regularly writing to his aunt who performed the work of an unpaid research assistant.

> Is it possible for an ordinary person to climb over the area railings of No 7 Eccles street, either from the path or the steps, lower himself down from the lower part of the railings till his feet are within 2 feet or 3 of the ground and drop unhurt ... I require this information in detail in order to determine the working of a paragraph.

Like every other work of Joyce's, *Ulysses* was entirely written by hand.

Nine typists failed in the attempt to transcribe the Circe episode from Joyce's undecipherable handwriting, which Beach considered 'as difficult to read as ogham' (an ancient Irish alphabet inscribed on stone).

The tenth typist also failed for different reasons. Sylvia Beach reported that:

> Her friend's husband had picked up the manuscript she was copying and, after one glance at it, had thrown it into the fire.

In the summer of 1921 the French literary critic and novelist Valery Larbaud lent the Joyce family his elegant, clean bachelor flat. It was there that the final chapter of *Ulysses*, in the voice of Molly Bloom, was written. During this time the writer suffered an attack of iritis so painful that he rolled around on the floor weeping. The doctor injected cocaine into his eyes and ordered him to cut his working hours from ten to six a day. By then Joyce was suffering from glaucoma, iritis, cataracts, nebula in the pupil, conjunctivitis, dissolution of the retina and abscesses. He had one-tenth of normal vision.

Nora was concerned but also furious, blaming James' drinking habits.

Harriet Weaver was alarmed too by stories about the writer's wild drinking binges, perhaps wondering if her generous patronage was encouraging alcoholism rather than literature. When she expressed her concerns to Joyce, he wrote back at length, making light of her doubts:

> Dear Miss Weaver,
>
> A nice collection could be made of legends about me … Triestines circulated the rumour, now firmly believed, that I am a cocaine victim … Somebody said of me here: 'They call him a poet. He appears to be interested chiefly in mattresses.' And, in fact, I was … The task I set myself technically in writing a book from eighteen different points of view and in as many styles … would be enough to upset anyone's mental balance … After that I want a good long rest in which to forget Ulysses completely.

In the first week of June 1921 Joyce wrote to his friend Francini Bruni excitedly:

> The book is already in press and I expect the first proofs day after tomorrow ... On the material side I think if the edition goes well (subscriptions come every day – three today from Australia) I will receive between 100,00 and 150,000 [lire].

The printer, located in Dijon, was still receiving new material to be inserted at the last minute. The proofs were so scribbled on that Joyce claimed that a third of the book was written in the margins.

In December, the first public reading of *Ulysses*, translated by Larbaud, was held in the Shakespeare and Company bookshop. The program for the event offered a trigger warning:

> *Nous tenons á prévenir le public que certaines des pages qu'on lira sont d'une hardiesse peu commune qui peut trés légitimement cheqoer.*

> The audience is warned that certain pages to be read are bolder than is common and might justly offend hearers.

## — 41 —

The first printing of *Ulysses* consisted of 1000 numbered copies. The first hundred, priced at 350 francs, were printed on Holland handmade paper and signed by Joyce; copies 101 to 250, priced at 250 francs, were printed on Arches paper, a special brand of air-dried paper made in the French village of Arches; the remaining 750 copies, priced at 150 francs, were printed on linen paper.

At Joyce's bidding, *Ulysses* was published by Shakespeare and Company on the second day of the second month of the twenty-second year of the twentieth century: the day he turned forty.

Joyce chose the cover to match what he called the 'Hellenic blue' of the Greek flag. He wrote to a friend:

> The colours of the binding (chosen by me) will be white letters on a blue field – the Greek flag though really of Bavarian origin and imported with the dynasty. Yet in a special way they symbolise the myth well – the white islands scattered over the sea.

One of Joyce's nicknames for Ulysses was

the Greco-Bavarian telephone directory.

Joyce and Beach did not trust the postal service so the first two copies were sent from the printer on the Dijon–Paris express train, arriving in Paris at 7am on the author's birthday. Beach met the train and took one copy to Joyce and the other to exhibit in the window of her bookshop. By mid-morning, subscribers were lining up outside.

Joyce gave the first copy of the limited edition to

Nora. She did not read it. When he gave her a later edition, he added a note:

> The edition you have is full of printers'
> errors. Please read it in this. I cut the pages.
> There is a list of mistakes at the end.
> Jim

He later commented to a friend:

> Nora has got as far as page 27, counting the
> cover.

On Joyce's birthday an employee of the London branch of the Bank of Australasia, (now the Australia and New Zealand Banking group ANZ), wrote to Sylvia Beach requesting a copy of the cheapest edition of *Ulysses* to be sent by registered post to Adelaide for Ronald Finlayson, solicitor and patron of the Adelaide Repertory Theatre. This was possibly the first copy of *Ulysses* to arrive in Australia.

Another first edition made its way to Toorak in Melbourne in 1922. It was bought by Fred Bryant, a regular traveller to Europe, for ten pounds and 10 shillings. By August he had decided to donate it to the then Melbourne Public Library.

Within weeks of the first publication, the cheapest edition of *Ulysses* had sold out.

A second edition of 2000 copies was published, some of which were shipped from Dijon to Dover, where they were seized and burned.

Copies that arrived at the port of New York were confiscated. Sylvia Beach arranged for a shipment to Canada where a friend of Hemingway's undertook to smuggle them across the border by stuffing copies down his pants.

Following the successful publication of *Ulysses*, crowds of writers, including D. H. Lawrence, flocked to Shakespeare and Company, assuming Beach was going to specialise in erotic fiction. Among others, she turned down *Lady Chatterley's Lover*.

As usual, Joyce was supremely confident about the value of his work, writing to his aunt about the copy of *Ulysses* he had sent to her:

> The market price of the book now in London is £40 and copies signed are worth more. I mention this because Alice told me you had lent it (or given?) and people in Dublin have a way of not returning books. In a few years copies of the first edition will probably be worth £100 each, so book experts say ...

In 2009, number 45 of the first edition sold at London's Antiquarian Book Show for £275,000. It was unopened, except for the last 'dirty' chapter.

Joyce eagerly awaited reviews and press coverage of his book. In England the reviews were so few that he concluded that there was a deliberate boycott.

*Ulysses* divided opinion.

Ezra Pound announced that the publication of

*Ulysses* heralded a new era in human history.

Virginia Woolf believed that *Ulysses* was:

> An illiterate, underbred book ...: the book of a self-taught working man, & we all know how distressing they are, how egotistic, insistent, raw, striking, & ultimately nauseating.

George Orwell reflected:

> When you read certain passages of *Ulysses* you feel that Joyce's mind and your mind are one, that he knows about you though he has never heard your name, that there exists some world outside time and space in which you and he are together.

Australian satirist John Clarke had similar feelings about the experience of reading Joyce:

> When I first came across Joyce I felt I was reading something that I felt in tune with – without knowing, at that stage, anything about being Irish or being Catholic. I was very struck with the ease with which I could identify with Stephen. It read as if it was written in the time I was living in. One of the things that Joyce encourages you to do, I think, is to be yourself, to find out who you are.

WB Yeats never finished *Ulysses*. His first impression was that it was 'a mad book'. Later, he said:

> It is perhaps a work of genius ... an entirely

new thing – neither what the eye sees nor the ear hears, but what the rambling mind thinks and imagines from moment to moment. He has certainly surpassed in intensity any novelist of our time.

Yeats was right. What Joyce was trying to do was replicate the rambling mind. His intention was nothing less than to document the experiential nature of consciousness.

In Australia, the critiques of *Ulysses* came largely from England. The Brisbane's *Telegraph* published a column headed 'From London Town' which quoted famous English critic Arnold Bennett's summation of *Ulysses* as 'this great bulk of filth', and Perth's *Daily News* reported on a lecture given to the Royal Society of Literature in London in which

> the well-known poet Mr Alfred Noyes opined that *Ulysses* was 'simply the foulest book that has ever made its way into print – there is not foulness conceivable to the mind of madman or ape that has not been poured into its imbecile pages … a corrupt mass of indescribable degradation'.

The Melbourne's *Herald*, however, offered an alternative view from psychiatrist and literary critic Reg Ellery, who announced that Joyce had written 'the first emancipated novel'.

Joyce was disappointed with what he considered

to be the pomposity and solemnity of much of the criticism of *Ulysses*. He felt the critics had missed the point, and he wished that more of them had realised that *Ulysses* was essentially a funny book. Years afterwards he reflected:

> I laugh at it today, now that I have had all the good of it. Let the bridge blow up, provided I have got my troops across ... nevertheless, that book was a terrible risk. A transparent leaf separates it from madness.

Madness was not only a theme in Joyce's work; it would also become his primary preoccupation, along with *Finnegans Wake*, for the rest of his life.

## — 42 —

Upon the publication of her husband's long-awaited book, Nora grew accustomed to people asking her if she was Molly. She would answer:

No, she was much fatter.

In the wake of the success of *Ulysses*, Nora finally saw an opportunity to take a break from her role as constant support and muse. She longed to return to Ireland and see her mother and after much resistance from Joyce, who was alarmed by the potentially violent political unrest in his homeland, Nora left with the children for a trip to Galway. Giorgio was seventeen,

Lucia fifteen.

Nora and the children spent some time in London on their way to Dublin. It appears that Joyce was frightened she might leave him for good. While there, he wrote to her:

> If you wish to live there (as you ask me to send two pounds a week) I will send that amount on the first of every month. Evidently it is impossible to describe to you the despair I have been in since you left. Yesterday I got a fainting fit in Miss Beach's shop ... my undying unhappy love.

In Ireland there was unrest. A treaty had been signed with Britain to partition the island into what Joyce called *Irrland's split little pea* and trouble was brewing between pro- and anti-treaty parties.

In Galway, Giorgio and Lucia were unimpressed by their grandmother's terrace house that smelled of boiled cabbage, so the family moved to a boarding house on nearby Nun's Island. A few days later, the IRA rushed in and mounted machine guns at their bedroom windows. It was then that Nora understood Joyce's warnings about violence had been valid. She decided, much to his relief, that she and the children had to return to Paris. On the way back to Dublin the train was set upon by snipers and they were again caught in crossfire. Nora would never return to her homeland.

Back in Paris, Lucia embarked on dance lessons at the Émile Jacques-Dalcroze's eurhythmics Institute.

Joyce's eyesight continued to worsen. Ezra Pound urged him to consult a well-known endocrinologist who was visiting Paris. The doctor also looked at the patient's teeth and advised complete extraction. Joyce underwent oral surgery and had seventeen teeth, seven abscesses and a cyst removed. He was installed with a complete set of false teeth.

## — 43 —

In 1923, *Thom's Irish Who's Who,* a publication that listed prominent Irishmen and women at home and abroad, did not include James Joyce's name.

## — 44 —

Less than a year after *Ulysses* was published, the idea for *Finnegans Wake* was forming.

Joyce wrote to Harriet Weaver:

> Yesterday I wrote two pages – the first I have written since the final Yes of *Ulysses*.

So began *Work in Progress*, the name given to his final book while drafting it.

For the next seventeen years the real title remained strictly secret, known only to himself and Nora.

Joyce's biggest fear was that he would go blind before he could finish it.

When the lease on their flat in Paris expired in June 1923, James and Nora decided to go on a summer holiday at the seaside and chose Bognor Regis, near Brighton, in England. In preparation, Joyce packed ten cases of books and three sacks of newspapers. While holidaying he came across a headstone in a graveyard with the name Earwicker. This would become the name of the family at the centre of *Finnegans Wake*.

Harriet Weaver gave Joyce another gift, this time of £12,000. The total amount she had transferred to the writer amounted to more than a million in contemporary Australian dollars.

On their return to Paris, the Joyces took up residence at the Grand Hotel, where Katherine Mansfield and John Middleton Murry had lived the year before. For a desk, Joyce used the surface of a green suitcase he had bought in Bognor.

Giorgio attended the Scuola Cantorum to study voice while Lucia returned to her study of dance. Both son and daughter were hoping to follow their father and become artists.

Joyce continued to drink to excess, often with Ernest Hemingway, while Nora continued to threaten to leave him and take the children back to Ireland.

Joyce employed a typist to transcribe an early

episode from *Work in Progress*.

> Dear Miss Bollach,
>
> After our interview the other evening it seems to me very unfair of me to have inflicted on you such difficult work. It is very kind of you to undertake but I think you are doing so at too great a sacrifice ... However as you are doing this piece may I ask you to make this one addition? ...
>
> With many apologies and kind regards sincerely yours,
>
> James Joyce.

## — 45 —

In early 1924 Joyce wrote to a friend about *Work in Progress*:

> The task I have set myself is dreadfully difficult but I believe it can be done. O dear me! What sins did I commit in my last incarnation to be in this hole?

Ford Maddox Ford, then editor of a new monthly bilingual magazine, the *transatlantic review,* published the first fragment from *Work in Progress,* known as the Mamalujo episode – Joyce's shorthand for the four evangelists Matthew, Mark, Luke and John.

The episode features the four men listening to the adulterous Tristan and Isolde kissing while also remembering nostalgically their own young romances:

> And so they were spraining their ears listening
> and listening to the oceans of kissening with
> their eyes glistening ...

Soon after he reported to Harriet Shaw Weaver that he had been working ten hours a day 'in semi-dark' and had suffered a 'nervous collapse', adding that:

> The Shaun the Post piece is very amusing –
> to me at least. It is extremely hard to write.

The Shaun the Post piece describes the immense appetite of the character Shaun, who was *guilbey of gulpable gluttony*, by listing what he ate at one sitting:

> his breakfast of first, a bless us O blood and
> thirsthy orange, next, the half of a pint of
> becon with newled googs and a segment of
> riceplummy padding, met of sunder suigar
> and some cold forsoaken steak peatrefired
> from the batblack night o'erflown then,
> without prejudice to evectuals, came along
> merendally his stockpot dinner of a half a
> pound of round steak very rare, Blong's best
> from Portarlington's Butchery with a side
> of ricepypeasy and Corkshire alla mellonge
> and bacon with (a little mar pliche!) a pair of
> chops and thrown in from the silver grid by
> the proprietoress of the roastery who lives on
> the hill and gaulusch gravy and pumpernickel
> to wolp up ...

Sometimes Joyce found his own writing so amusing that he kept Nora awake with his guffaws of laughter.

## — 46 —

In late 1924, Joyce wrote to Sylvia Beach, after yet another operation for his diminishing eyesight, referring to his left eye as 'the broken window of my soul'.

## — 47 —

January 19th, 1925
Dear Miss Bollach,
If you are not too busy I should be much obliged if you could type some more of my incomprehensible MS.

A month later, Joyce's eye pain became so severe that he was administered morphine.

His eyesight was so poor that Lucia was writing her father's letters for him.

April 1st, 1925
Dear Miss Bollach,
Please write back with a heavy black pencil.
I cannot distinguish one word of print or pen but can pencil with a magnifying glass.

In May, another extract from what would become *Finnegans Wake* was published in *Contact Collection* of *Contemporary Writers,* alongside pieces by Ernest Hemingway and Gertrude Stein. This fragment introduced the principal male character, Humphrey Chimpden Earwicker.

In July, a further episode, introducing the main female character, Anna Livia Plurabelle, was published in the British literary magazine, *Criterion* (Issue III) established and edited by T. S. Eliot.

> *In the name of Annah the Allmaziful, the Everliving, the Bringer of Plurabilities, hallowed be here ever, her singtime sung, her rill be run, unhemmed as it is uneven.*

Joyce wrote to Weaver, to whom he had promised the final original handwritten manuscript of *Work in Progress* as a gift:

> Your MS this time will be partly written by Lucia …

By the end of 1925, Lucia was not only acting as Joyce's secretary, she was also occasionally transcribing *Work in Progress.* The extent of her influence on the final work is the subject of much conjecture. Carl Jung would later call Lucia her father's 'inspiratrice'.

## – **48** –

When Joyce sent Ezra Pound an extract from *Work in Progress,* he responded:

Dear Jim,

MS arrived this a.m. I make nothing of it
whatever. Nothing so far as I make out,
nothing short of divine vision or a new cure
for the clap can possibly be worth all the
circumambient peripherization.

In an effort to explain his new writing style, Joyce
wrote to Weaver, intimating that he was trying to
recreate the reality of a dream:

One great part of every human existence is
passed in a state which cannot be rendered
sensible by the use of wideawake language,
cutanddry grammar and goahead plot.

In June, he wrote again to Miss Bollach thanking
her for the latest revision of *Work in Progress.*

Will you please let me know how many hours
of dreadful labour it cost you?

In December 1926, Joyce invited a few select
friends to his apartment to hear a recitation of the
opening pages of *Work in Progress,* having realised
perhaps that his new style was more easily understood
through performance than reading. Afterwards he fell
into a state of complete exhaustion, describing it later
in a letter to Weaver as 'a first class collapse'.

In early 1927, Joyce became deeply depressed by the uncomprehending response to his *Work in Progress* and considered abandoning his book altogether. He was further depressed by the publication of a pirated edition of *Ulysses* in the the United States.

He was invited to London to be a guest of honour at the dinner of the PEN Club, writing to Weaver that he was

> patching up my wardrobe in order to look like a respectable litteratoor when I sit down at the dinner table.

Once seated, he became annoyed that the conversation was dominated by discussion of politics rather than literature.

A petition of protest against the pirated edition of *Ulysses* was signed, among others, by E. M. Forster, Thomas Mann, Somerset Maugham, Gabriel Miró, Virginia Woolf and Einstein.

In July, *Pomes Penyeach,* Joyce's second collection of poetry, was published by Shakespeare and Company. A further extract from *Work in Progress* was published in a newly established literary magazine, *transition,* which according to Joyce attracted 'more kilos of abuse'. He nevertheless continued work on the next extract, writing to Weaver in October that he had:

just finished revision of Anna Livia for
transition No. 8. What a job! 1200 hours of
work on 17 pages.

In December, the United States Supreme Court
ordered Samuel Roth, the publisher responsible for the
piracy of *Ulysses*, to stop using Joyce's name in any
way.

## — 50 —

In early 1928, Joyce wrote to a friend that he'd

had the worst Xmas and New Year I can
remember … painfully ill – with inflammation
of intestines – caused by overwork and worry.

After writing one of his many letters to Weaver
outlining his woes – his own illnesses as well as Nora's
serious gynecological problems – Joyce added:

Lucia dances through it all.

Among Lucia's many dance mentors was Raymond
Duncan, brother of Isadora, and Margaret Morris,
the founder of the Scottish National Ballet and
granddaughter of the famous nineteenth century
designer, William Morris.

## — 51 —

In January 1928 Weaver became deeply unnerved
by the drafts of Joyce's new book and feared he was

wasting his genius. She was so concerned that she arranged a trip to Paris to speak with him. Joyce spent many hours explaining his new writing methods and she returned to London reassured.

Another extract from *Work in Progress*, 'The Ondt and the Gracehoper', was published in *transition*. It was clear that Joyce identified more with the grasshopper of the fable than the ant.

> The Gracehoper was always jigging ajog,
> hoppy on akkant of his joyicity …

Back in Paris after their summer away, Joyce endured another serious eye attack and collapsed. By then his weight had dropped to eight stone (51 kg).

## — 52 —

At the age of twenty-one, Lucia's dance career looked exceptionally promising. Her sister-in-law described her as a 'gifted child of a gifted father'. Following a 1928 performance at the La Princesse Primitive at the Vieux-Colombier theatre, the *Paris Times* remarked: 'When she reaches her full capacity for rhythmic dancing, James Joyce may yet be known as his daughter's father.'

In May 1929, Lucia was a finalist at the first Paris international festival of dance. She wore a shimmering silver fish costume covered in scales that she had designed herself.

Afterwards one of the judges noted that the young *Irlandaise* was the only contestant with the potential to be a professional dancer. Joyce was annoyed, however, when his daughter was awarded only second place, perhaps reminding him of his own second place in the 1904 Feis Ceoil Tenor competition at the age of twenty-two. Like her father, who had promptly dropped his musical aspirations due to his runner-up status, Lucia abruptly gave up on modernist, avant-garde dance and turned instead to classical ballet, studying six hours a day with a stern and merciless teacher, Lubov Egorova, who had originally come to Paris with the Russian ballet.

Lucia's pursuit of physical expression on stage had mixed family support and by October 1929 she had decided, with Joyce's approval, to give up dancing as a professional pursuit. According to Lucia's sister-in-law, Lucia's sudden decision was not altogether voluntary but rather she was 'nagged and bullied' by her mother until she gave up. One observer opined that it was Lucia's success as a dancer, rather than her failure, that created discord in the Joyce household. Perhaps a cramped apartment did not have room for two highly strung artists.

Another observer believed that Joyce had impressed upon Lucia that it was 'unseemly for women to get on the stage and wave their arms about'. 'Unseemly', or *unzeimlich*, was also the word Leopold Mozart used to dissuade his daughter Nannerl – who was very possibly as talented as her younger brother Wolfgang – from performing publicly.

This sacrifice of Lucia's artistic passion appears to be the beginning of her descent into mental instability.

## – 53 –

By 1929 Samuel Beckett had became a regular visitor to the Joyce household, and yet another devoted member of the hard-working team behind the production of the great writer's work, occasionally transcribing parts of *Finnegans Wake* as Joyce dictated. On one occasion, in response to a knock at the door, Joyce said, 'Come in,' and Beckett dutifully added 'Come in' to the dictated text. Joyce decided to let it stand. He was always willing, says Ellmann,

to accept coincidence as his collaborator.

## – 54 –

A collection of essays reflecting on *Work in Progress*, with authors such as Samuel Beckett and William Carlos Williams, was published by Shakespeare and Company in May 1929. *Our Exagmination Round his Factification for Incamination of Work in Progress* has been described as an apologia for Joyce's seemingly incomprehensible prose. In it a letter appeared which allegedly had been delivered to Sylvia Beach's bookshop by an unknown hand; it was the first parody of *Finnegans Wake*:

> Dear Mister Germ's Choice,
>
> in gutter dispear I am taking my pen toilet you know that, being Leyde up in bad with the prewailent distemper (I opened the window and in flew Enza), I have been reeding one half ter one other the numboars of 'transition' in witch are printed the severeall instorments of your 'Work in Progress'... I am writing you, dear mysterr Shame's Voice, to let you no how bed I feeloxerab out it all.

Some Joyceans believe the letter was written by Joyce himself.

## — 55 —

In relation to her daughter's continuing agitated state, Nora is reported to have remarked:

> What Lucia needs is a nice young husband.

Lucia put it differently, describing herself as sex-starved.

Joyce embarked on a campaign to get his daughter married off, believing that this would be a solution to her increasingly bizarre behaviour. Perhaps there was still a belief that hysteria was related to the womb and that any womanly anxiety could be alleviated by the bearing of children.

The first marriage candidate was Samuel Beckett with whom Lucia had become infatuated. Beckett was 23. She was 21. On first meeting with Lucia, Beckett recognised that the great writer's daughter had something of her father's genius and initially he was attracted by Lucia's electric energy. For her part, she was clearly thrilled to receive attention from one of her father's most ardent admirers and claimed she could see their future life together. But when she declared her love to him, Beckett became alarmed and felt obliged to announce bluntly that his visits to the apartment were to see her father, not her. On hearing this, Lucia reportedly 'lapsed into a catatonic state'. Later she was to comment that the men who came to their home treated her like a 'hors d'oeuvre'. Years later, Beckett confessed to his lover Peggy Guggenheim that he:

> had no feelings that were human and this is why he had not been able to fall in love with Joyce's daughter.

## — 56 —

Throughout 1930, Joyce worked intensely on *Finnegans Wake*.

Giorgio developed a relationship with Helen Kastor Fleischmann, a recently divorced American heiress, eleven years his senior. Biographers speculate that she was more interested in Joyce than in Giorgio. Helen soon became an enthusiastic part of the team devoted to *Work in Progress*. She regularly read aloud long extracts from the *Encyclopaedia Britannica*, one of the many texts Joyce drew from.

In many ways Joyce's final work is an anti-encyclopaedia, opposed to the kind of system of knowledge that is presented as linear and alphabetical. But if it is not offering the conventional system of knowledge, and it's not a conventional novel, then what is it? *Finnegans Wake* has been described as many things:

> a mighty allegory of the fall and resurrection of mankind;
>
> an ark to contain all human myths and types;
>
> a polyhedron of scripture;
>
> a postmodern encyclopaedia;
>
> the most profoundly antifascist book produced between the wars;
>
> an Irish word ballet;
>
> a Wholesale Safety Pun Factory;
>
> an immense poem of sleep;
>
> an engagement with the very matter of our being;
>
> a history of the world;
>
> a history of the future.

Joyce said that history was like a parlour game where someone whispers something to the next person who repeats it not very distinctly to the next person, and so on, until, by the time the last person hears it, it comes out completely transformed and corrupted. This is partly why he puts so much importance on gossip, or, as he calls it, 'gossiple'.

## — 57 —

In May 1930, a ninth operation was performed on Joyce's left eye for a tertiary cataract. The growth was cut through horizontally but complications meant that the surgery could not be completed. A week later, leeches were applied to remove blood that had accumulated behind the eyeball.

> June: Report by Dr Alfred Vogt
>
> It has been decided to defer the tenth operation till middle of September 1930. The operation just performed will probably produce a slight amelioration of vision in the left eye which before had a seeing power of 1/800 to 1/1000.
>
> Right eye: still presents a complicated cataract on which an eleventh operation must ultimately be performed.

Joyce's eyesight was now so bad that he could not walk into a room and be sure to avoid bumping into furniture. He could only read very large type with glasses and two magnifying glasses. He would later take to wearing white linen because he believed it reflected any given light.

On June 15 the Anna Livia Plurabelle episode from *Work in Progress* was published by Faber & Faber, whom Joyce called 'Feebler and Feebler', as *Criterion Miscellany No. 15*. The price was one shilling.

The episode begins with two washerwomen gossiping on a riverbank:

<blockquote>
O<br>
tell me all about<br>
Anna Livia! I want to hear all<br>
about Anna Livia! Well, you know Anna<br>
Livia ...
</blockquote>

## — 58 —

In December 1930, Giorgio married Helen Fleischmann. No longer needing to earn a living, his interest in a singing career began to wane.

## — 59 —

In May 1931, the 'Haveth Childers Everywhere' episode from *Work in Progress* was published by Faber & Faber as *Criterion Miscellany No. 26*.

Haveth Childers Everywhere is another name for Humphrey Chimpden Earwicker. Like all the characters in *Finnegans Wake*, his identity is constantly shifting and he appears in the book under hundreds of different names, including Happiest Childer Everwere, Humpty Dumpty, Hombreyhambrey, Howth Castle and Environs, Helviticus committed Deuteronomy, Haroun Childeric Eggeberth, He'll Cheat E'erawan, and Here Comes Everybody.

As with so many things, Joyce was ahead of his time in relation to fluid identities. He even invented a pronoun that melded she, he and they.

> *youthsy, beautsy, hee's her chap and shey'll tell memmas when she gays whom*

Joyce wrote rhymes for the purpose of publicising the Anna Livia Plurabelle and HCE episodes but the sales manager declined to utilise them. The ALP rhyme was as follows:

> Buy a book in brown paper
> From Faber & Faber
> To see Annie Liffey trip, tumble and caper.
> Sevensinns in her singthings,
> Plurabelle on her prose,
> Seeshell ebb music wayriver she flows.

# — 60 —

In June 1931 Joyce wrote rapturously to Lucia after seeing the Indian dancer Uday Shankar (brother of Ravi):

> He moves on the stage floor like a semi-divine being. Altogether, believe me, there are still some beautiful things in this poor old world.

Joyce himself had a fondness of dancing. His daughter-in-law, Helen, said:

> Liquor went to his feet, not his head.

And Joyce's close friend Budgen reported that:

> on festive occasions Joyce would execute a fantastic dance ... a thing of whirling arms and highkicking legs that suggested somehow the ritual antics of a comic religion.

It is a mystery why he shared his love of dancing with Lucia and yet apparently did not encourage her desire to dance professionally.

# — 61 —

In the summer of 1931, the Joyce family, now consisting of James, Nora and Lucia, went to London and took up residence in Campden Grove, Kensington, intending to stay for six months.

On 4 July, Joyce and Nora Barnacle were married

at the registry office in Kensington, an event that attracted a good deal of media attention. Joyce's opposition to the institution of marriage had not changed but he had become convinced that, for the purpose of his literary estate, it was necessary to formalise his relationship with Nora.

It came as a shock to Lucia that she had been born an illegitimate child and she was upset by her parents' marriage. She decided to leave England in August to join her brother and sister-in-law in Paris.

Joyce quickly realised that the English cottage lifestyle was not for him and later he would refer to their location as Campden Grave. In September, Nora and Joyce followed their daughter back to Paris for the winter, planning to return to England the following spring.

In December 1931, Joyce's father died.

The news left Joyce so grief-stricken that he again considered abandoning work on *Finnegans Wake* altogether. He wrote to Harriet Shaw Weaver (who would pay for John Joyce's funeral):

> I got from him an extravagant licentious disposition (out of which, however, the greatest part of any talent I may have springs). I was very fond of him always, being a sinner myself, and even liked his faults. Hundreds of pages and scores of characters in my books came from him.

During his deep bereavement, Joyce devised a new calendar of weekdays:

> Moansday
> Tearsday
> Wailsday
> Thumpsday
> Frightday
> Shatterday

## — 62 —

In 1932, Joyce's fiftieth birthday was marred when his daughter threw a chair at Nora in an outburst of fury.

This may have been Lucia's first psychotic break. A taxi was called to take her to the nearby *maison de santé*.

That evening Joyce was so upset that even the sight of his jubilee birthday cake, complete with fifty candles and a replica in sugar of *Ulysses*, did not cheer him up.

Two weeks later, his mood was lifted when Helen gave birth to Joyce's first and only grandchild, who was named Stephen after Stephen Dedalus.

## — 63 —

When their lease on their apartment expired in April 1932, the family packed up yet again to leave for

London. While waiting at the Gard du Nord train station, Lucia caused a loud and dramatic scene, screaming that she hated England, and refused to board the train.

Joyce recounted to a friend:

> Lucia had a bad *crise de nerfs* at the Gare du Nord … So here we are in a hotel again, after 12 years in Paris.

Nora blamed their itinerant existence for Lucia's unsettled temperament and this time went as far as packing her suitcases with the intention of leaving him.

Stuart Gilbert, a close friend and the only eyewitness to the train station episode, observed in his diary:

> The truth is that none of the family wanted to go.

He reflected that after Lucia had settled down, they were all quite happy to surrender the plan and go to lunch in a nearby restaurant. Later, Gilbert hypothesised that Lucia had acted out of neuroses that belonged to her parents – giving expression to what they found impossible to express. Gilbert did not believe Lucia was insane, but considered her 'theatricality' simply a result of her need to be the object of attention.

Following the railway incident, Joyce resigned himself to having to consult doctors about his daughter, although he defiantly rejected their diagnoses. According to Richard Ellmann, it was from this moment that a gloom settled on Joyce 'of almost tragic dimensions'.

Giorgio, convinced that his sister was mad, escorted her to the sanatorium of Dr Gaston Maillard at l'Hay-les-Roses without telling her where they were going.

Dr Maillard's diagnosis was that Lucia was suffering from 'hebephrenic psychosis with serious prognosis', a form of schizophrenia. The word 'schizophrenia' had been in existence for little more than thirty years and had previously been referred to as *dementia praecox* – premature dementia.

In Greek mythology, Hebe is the goddess of youth or the prime of life, the Roman equivalent to Juventas. Hence, hebephrenia is related to a type of psychosis that arises in young people.

Dr Maillard's prescription for Lucia's malady was solitary confinement and that she stay in bed for several weeks.

## – 64 –

In one of a series of letters written to Harriet Weaver by Joyce's devoted friend Paul Léon it was reported that 'the effect of his daughter's health' was having a tremendous impact on the writer's nerves and referred to Lucia's 'relapse' as being the reason for his 'recent collapse'.

I consider his recent second breakdown as a second warning which should not be lightly overlooked.

Weaver's own observation of Joyce during her visit to Paris was that his periodic collapses were probably more likely due to his drinking habits. Léon, presumably under Joyce's direction, went out of his way to convince Weaver otherwise.

> ... [which] brings me to the allusion you made in your letter. I mean drinking ... I made a special point to bring in the conversation with the doctor this matter. Dr. Debray is resolutely and absolutely of the opinion that drink has nothing to do with his collapse ... the principal worry by far overshadowing all other problems has been the state of health of his daughter.

The letter ends emphatically:

> I do think Mr Joyce belongs to his work and unless he is able to do it he will not get well.

The cost of Lucia's healthcare was also another major preoccupation. Joyce, like his once-wealthy father, had gradually sold off the stock gifted to him by Weaver, spending much of it on his daughter. This shocked Weaver because her intention had been for him to live off the interest and leave the principal untouched.

## — 65 —

Joyce was not convinced that the treatment from the l'Hay-les-Roses clinic was making Lucia better, writing to a friend:

> Things are not going well. They have even proposed that my daughter be kept in total isolation, an idea my whole nature revolts against.

Within weeks he had smuggled her out.

Joyce told himself that his difficulties with writing his final work were in parallel with his daughter's turmoil. He tried to convince himself that once he emerged out of his book of the dark, Lucia would also recover. He confided to a friend:

> Sometimes I tell myself that when I leave this dark night, she too will be cured.

## — 66 —

In July 1933 Joyce took Lucia to Zurich to see Europe's preeminent authority on schizophrenia, Professor Maier, chief physician of the mental asylum at Burgholzli. Maier's view was that Lucia was 'not a lunatic but markedly neurotic' and advised that she should be placed in the Les Rives de Prangins sanatorium in Nyon, just outside Geneva. Prangins was Europe's foremost facility for the wealthy mentally ill, where Zelda Fitzgerald had spent time in 1931. It continues to operate as a psychiatric facility to this day and is now known as the Hôpital de Prangins.

At Prangins, Lucia received the diagnosis of 'schizophrenia with pithiatric elements'. Pithiatric is an obsolete term meaning 'capable of being cured by persuasion and suggestion'. Six days later, however, she appeared so unhappy that Joyce decided to take her back home again.

## – 67 –

In December 1933 *Ulysses* was again the subject of obscenity charges in the United States. The case had been brought against the book and not against the publisher, the importer or the author.

*United States v. One Book Called Ulysses*

Court cases against things are called *in rem jurisdiction*. Other court cases against things include:

*United States v. One Tyrannosaurus Bataar Skeleton*

*United States v. One Package of Japanese Pessaries*

*United States v. Thirty-seven Photographs*

*United States v. One Buick Oldsmobile*

Judge John M. Woolsey, a United States District Judge, decided that the book was dirty but that it was not 'dirt for dirt's sake', describing it as 'a somewhat tragic but very powerful commentary on the inner lives of men and women'. He ruled that *Ulysses* was not pornographic as it would make people nauseous rather than lustful. It was therefore not obscene.

When the news spread about the court's decision, the Joyces' phone rang constantly with calls of congratulations.

Lucia's response was to cut the phone wires, saying:

*C'est moi qui est l'artiste.*
It's me who is the artist.

When they were repaired she cut them again.

## — 68 —

Many friends and colleagues of Joyce's believed that the most important thing was that the great writer be allowed to pursue his work. To do that, he needed to be rid of his difficult daughter.

In January 1934 Lucia ran away from home for three days before being brought back by the police. She was again institutionalised in Prangins where she was kept under restraint, often locked up in solitary confinement with barred windows and was constantly under surveillance.

Lucia attempted to escape Prangins several times,

once getting as far as the French border. Finally, she set fire to the tablecloth in her cell in a bid to be released.

## — 69 —

*Ulysses* was finally legally published in the United States, coinciding with the repeal against Prohibition. This prompted one of Joyce's allies to remark that minds and bottles had been opened at the same time.

Joyce wrote to his friend Budgen that *Ulysses* had sold 33,000 copies in ten weeks in the United States.

In May 1934 Giorgio and his wife Helen left for the United States, partly under the pretext that it would be good for Giorgio's singing career. Joyce wrote to his son, encouraging him in his pursuit of a musical career, and advising him on his diction:

> Think of the words, I entreat you. Singing is only language with wings.

For the first time in nearly thirty years, Nora and James were left alone together without children.

## — 70 —

Joyce devised a scheme to keep Lucia active and artistically engaged by proposing a creative collaboration. It would involve a special edition of his poetry collection *Pomes Penyeach*, which Lucia would illustrate. He hoped that this would keep her busy and possibly bring in some income.

Lucia, *the dotter of her father's eyes*, set to work on illustrating Joyce's words with *lettrines*, illustrated capital letters. She was to decorate the first letter of each poem. Under F was the poem 'A Flower Given to My Daughter':

> Frail the white rose and frail are
> Her hands that gave
> Whose soul is sere and paler
> Than time's wan wave.
>
> Rosefrail and fair – yet frailest
> A wonder wild
> In gentle eyes thou veilest,
> My blueveined child.

When the special edition was published, the art critic Louis Gillet, in a review for *Revue des deux mondes,* remarked that Lucia's *lettrines* were 'a marvel of atavism' and compared them with those of ancient Irish illuminators, such as appear in the *Book of Kells.*

Stuart Gilbert noted that: 'The neurotic Lucia seems to have quite recovered and is interested, above all, in her publicity. She has, I think, some talent.' The book, however, brought little profit.

In 2014, the opening bid at a New York auction for an original signed edition of *Pomes Penyeach* started at $61,000.

## — 71 —

Despite her father's devoted efforts, Lucia's mental health did not improve.

On the suggestion of Weaver, Lucia was taken to a new doctor by the name of Dr Vignes. His view was that Lucia had 'ruined her nervous system by five years dancing strain'. He prescribed injections of seawater. The treatment proved ineffective. Joyce again brought his daughter back to their apartment.

## — 72 —

Giorgio, still in the United States, was also suffering some undiagnosed illness. In a letter to his benefactor, Joyce wrote:

> Some strange malady has been creeping over both my children …

## — 73 —

Following years of rejecting the suggestion of psychoanalysis for Lucia, in 1934 Joyce finally relented to consulting the famous Swiss doctor, Carl Jung.

Jung was Lucia's twentieth doctor.

One of the reasons Joyce had resisted consulting Jung was because of the psychiatrist's public comments about *Ulysses*:

The whole work has the character of a worm cut in half, that can grow a new head or a new tail as required. This singular and uncanny characteristic of the Joycean mind shows that his work pertains to the class of cold-blooded animals and specifically to the worm family. If worms were gifted with literary powers they would write with the sympathetic nervous system for lack of a brain. I suspect that something of this kind has happened to Joyce, that here we have a case of visceral thinking with severe restrictions of cerebral activity and its confinement to the perceptual processes.

Joyce's response was:

He seems to have read *Ulysses* from first to last without a smile. The only thing to do in such a case is to change one's drink.

A friend remarked that the reason Carl Jung was so rude about Joyce was because Joyce's name translated into German as *freude*.

Joyce continued to insist that the problem with Lucia was that she was an innovator who was not yet understood. He commented to a friend:

People talk of my influence on my daughter but what about her influence on me? ... She is a fantastic being who speaks a curious abbreviated language of her own ... I understand it, or most of it.

It has been hypothesised that this curious language

inspired the curious language of *Finnegans Wake.*

After a few months, Jung concluded that Lucia was as unreadable as her father's famous book, and that Joyce was so solidly identified with Lucia that 'to have her certified would have been an admission that he himself had a latent psychosis'. He later wrote that Joyce and Lucia were a 'classical example' of his Anima theory.

## — 74 —

In 1935, the Australian journalist Leslie Rees wrote to Joyce asking if he and his wife Coralie Clarke Rees, also a journalist and a writer, could visit. They received a response via Paul Léon saying that Mr Joyce never saw the Press but might like to arrange a meeting on different grounds.

The couple were invited to Joyce's flat not far from the Eiffel Tower. Rees' account of the meeting describes Joyce as a 'thin nervous figure'.

> Joyce asked:
> So you are from Australia? I don't usually see people but you seemed to have come such a long way, I couldn't very well refuse you.

The couple 'immediately felt like imposters' because in fact they had come from London where had been living for several years. And then Joyce began asking 'numerous quiet questions about Australia'.

> What is the Australian accent? It always
> bothers me when they talk about it.

Joyce was fascinated by accents and he was bothered, perhaps, because the Australian accent was one of the few he'd never heard. Indeed, Joyce appeared to know a lot more about Australia than Australians knew about him. He was fascinated by the Southern Hemisphere, or *the antipathies* as he called it. In one of a cluster of passages in *Finnegans Wake* that focus on the colonialist game of cricket, he mentions twice a famous Aboriginal cricketer nicknamed Bullocky – who was part of an all-Indigenous team that toured England in 1868 – along with his teammate, Twopenny. Joyce also appears to have taken a special interest in Australian birdlife, referring to the Noisy Friarbird, native to New South Wales – *the friarbird. Listening, Syd!* – as well as the *cursowarries* and the extinct White Swamp Hen of New South Wales (Prophyrio Albus), which is mentioned in a footnote as *Porphyrious Olbion.*

Rees asked Joyce whether he wrote every day. He said he did if he was well enough, referring to his eyesight, adding:

> I cannot see you, sitting opposite me.

Rees had brought with him a copy of *Ulysses,* which he had hidden in his overcoat pocket while passing through British Customs Officers. As they took their leave, Joyce signed it 'a little reluctantly'. When asked if he was troubled by censorship of his books, he replied:

No, not bitter. Just bored.

Afterwards Rees wrote:

He seemed a man in eternal pain and, without complaining, he communicated his pain to us.

## — 75 —

When Lucia left Jung's clinic, Joyce and Nora disagreed on what to do next. Joyce wanted his daughter back in Paris, while Nora refused to have such a disruptive presence in the apartment. After all, the care of Lucia mostly fell to Nora as Joyce retreated to write.

Ellmann describes this period of Joyce's life as his 'nadir'. He couldn't sleep and experienced auditory hallucinations as well as severe stomach pain. When a doctor was consulted, Joyce was again told he was suffering from nerves. It seems clear that this intense state of anxiety was brought on by the stress of caring for Lucia.

Paul Léon, Joyce's constant and loyal assistant, wrote to Weaver:

Mr Joyce is constantly complaining of having

'not a morsel of strength left'.

Despite this, Joyce continued work on *Finnegans Wake*, often through the night until five in the morning. Nora referred to his latest work as 'that chop suey' and asked him:

> Why don't you write sensible books that people can understand?

After his death she changed her mind and would comment that she didn't understand what all the fuss was about *Ulysses* – that *Finnegans Wake* was the masterpiece.

## — 76 —

Joyce believed his genius had cast a shadow on Lucia's psyche, concluding:

> Whatever spark of gift I possess has been transmitted to Lucia and kindled a fire in her brain.

He wrote regularly to his daughter during her incarcerations in various institutions, usually in Italian:

> Cara Lucia:
> I feel more than ever, my poor, dear and good Lucia, that the long night of your travails is drawing to an end and that the dawn is coming.

Joyce's mood in the face of his daughter's condition belied his words. His friends observed that he seemed to be in complete despair and prone to 'lachrymose fits'.

Three-quarters of Joyce's income was now going to Lucia's care and he was at risk of financial ruin. When Joyce's sister in Ireland wrote to him offering lottery tickets as a way of alleviating his financial stress, he responded:

> I am not interested in Irish Sweepstake tickets. The only decent people I ever saw at a racecourse were the horses.

## — 77 —

*Finnegans Wake* is often described as a book written in dream language. For a long time the dreaming narrator was believed to be Humphrey Chimpden Earwicker.

Consistent with the madness theme of the *Wake,* the name Earwicker suggests the earwig, an insect which was so named because it was believed it could burrow into the brain of a sleeping person and cause insanity.

Of madness, Joyce once commented to his friend, painter and art critic Arthur Power:

> Madness you may call it ... I prefer the word

exaltation, exaltation which can merge into madness, perhaps. In fact all great men have had that vein in them; it was the source of their greatness; the reasonable man achieves nothing.

## — 78 —

Paul Léon, in a letter to Harriet Weaver, wrote:

Mrs Joyce told me he was in a state of exhaustion over the closing pages of the book which he had written in a state of extreme tension ... It is impossible to deny that he has acted according to his conscience and that he has actually consumed almost all of his substance, physical and spiritual, moral and material in the writing of a book likely to be received with derision by his ill-wishers and with pained displeasure by his friends.

The final passage of *Finnegans Wake* was allegedly sketched out in one afternoon, after which Joyce told his friend:

I felt so completely exhausted, as if all the blood had run out of my brain.

## — 79 —

When asked whether his *Work in Progress* was a blending of literature and music, Joyce replied:

No, it's pure music.

But are there not levels of meaning to be explored? the questioner pressed.

No, no, said Joyce, it's meant to make you laugh.

## — 80 —

In 1938 two American publishers offered an $11,000 advance and 20% royalties to publish *Finnegans Wake*. After seventeen years of writing and rewriting, drafting and redrafting, it was finally published by Faber and Faber in February 1939. Joyce only told the publishers the real title just before reaching the binding stage.

James Joyce's final work was received, with a few exceptions, with ridicule, incomprehension and bafflement. To F. R. Leavis, the most powerful English literary critic of the time, it was of 'monotonous insignificance'. *The Irish Times* mocked: 'And what of the middle portion of this work of art? There is no middle, either.' Even Joyce's younger brother, Stanislaus, said it was either the work of a psychopath or a huge literary fraud.

But others believed it was the work of a magician and that *Finnegans Wake* was a kind of magic spell, which was perhaps what Joyce believed too. Of Joyce's thoughts about *Finnegans Wake* the Joycean scholar J. S. Atherton noted:

He believed that his words were words of silent power ... that he was entrapping some part of the essence of life within the pages of *Finnegans Wake* – that somehow the spirit of language was working through him of its own volition ... Joyce was not simply writing a book, he was also performing a work of magic.

Even Australia's *Tweed Daily* hinted at the possible magical quality of the text at the same time as recoiling from it. Squeezed between advertisements for fertilisers and shrubs, the rural paper from Murwillumbah reported briefly:

Nonsense or Magic?

It may be that Mr Joyce is attempting to invent a new language which will have the suggestive quality of music rather than of literature – music at times comic and at times poetic ... Collectors, no doubt, will treasure the book as a curiosity. But to the ordinary reader it will remain a sealed book, and seem merely symptomatic of the chaos into which the modern world has fallen.

The *Sydney Morning Herald* discerned the latent 'madness' in Joyce's final book:

Readers might well be forgiven for having imagined that the whole thing was a monstrous joke, a barefaced attempt to impose on their intelligence the mixed dregs of languages as a true literary work ... it looks as though the

jester without taste or sense of measure is at
work; in other passages alienists have discerned
a plain lunatic. But the jester, the lunatic, is
man's own unconscious mind!

It was left to scholar and lecturer Alexander King
to explicate the book at length to Australian readers in
*The West Australian*, concluding:

> We need to give to this work the attention we
> give to great poetry, when we are willing to
> be worked upon and to gather up slowly the
> meaning of what is too complicated or subtle
> to be expressed in the plain prose Joyce-haters
> wish he would write. What Joyce has tried to
> give us is the night mind of man, the timeless
> adventures in sleep, not of one human mind,
> but the human mind.

## — 81 —

The incursion of madness in the Joyce family
continued. In 1939 Giorgio's wife, Helen, was
hospitalised in America after a mental breakdown. On
recovery, the couple returned to Paris but soon after
she appeared to be heading for another breakdown
and was hospitalised again. The couple separated and
their son Stephen was sent to a boarding school in
Saint-Gérand-le-Puy in rural France. Given the threat
of war, Lucia's *maison de santé* was planning to move
to a rural location but had not been able to secure one

anywhere. Joyce proposed hiring a car and travelling to the sanatorium to collect his daughter with the help of two nurses but the roads by then had been blocked. In the meantime, as the rest of the family decamped to Saint-Gérand-le-Puy, Joyce despaired:

> Lucia is therefore left alone in a Paris about to be bombed ...

# — 82 —

In December 1939, at a Christmas Eve dinner shared with family and friends, Joyce could scarcely eat as he was overcome with stomach pain which was again attributed to nerves. Towards the end of the evening, however, he had a burst of joyous energy and invited his hostess to dance, saying:

> You know very well it's the last Christmas.

In the weeks that followed his gloom returned. The poor reception of *Finnegans Wake* had depressed him and the fact that the threat of war had all but eclipsed his final work only added to his low spirits. He took to lapsing into silence for days. Nora commented to a guest:

> There sits a man who has not spoken one word to me all day.

# — 83 —

In 1940 Helen Fleischmann's brother came to Paris and, with the help of two nurses, escorted his sister back to the United States.

In June, Nazi Germany took Paris. Sylvia Beach shut her shop down rather than sell her last remaining copy of *Finnegans Wake* to a Nazi officer. She cleared out over 4,000 books, stripped all the shelves and painted over the sign above the door. When the officer returned there was no indication a bookshop had ever been there.

After months of intense bureaucratic wrangling with French and Swiss authorities, Joyce obtained visas for all the family to travel to Switzerland. However, by then Lucia's *permis de sortie* had expired, and the family had to leave without her.

The Joyce family packed their documents, a few suitcases and grandson Stephen's bicycle in preparation to travel by night train to Switzerland. They arrived safely in Geneva but without the bicycle, which was confiscated by Swiss authorities at the border because Joyce couldn't afford to pay the duty. From Geneva they went on to Lausanne and booked into a hotel. On unpacking, Nora discovered that her husband's green ink had spilt over everything inside their suitcase. His response was to send the young Stephen out for Swiss chocolate. That very afternoon,

Joyce went to the nearest *maison de santé* to arrange for Lucia's transfer.

Two days later the family packed up again and left for Zurich. Joyce, Nora, Giorgio and Stephen were met at the Hauptbahnhof by an old friend who later described them as looking

> like some of the angular figures in a Picasso drawing, huddled together on the platform. Their clothes had grown too large for them and hung loosely about their thin forms.

Back in Paris, the Joyces' landlord was selling the contents of their abandoned flat to pay for arrears of rent. Paul Léon managed to rescue some books and papers and bought other items at an illegal auction. He then took them to the Irish Ambassador with instructions that they should be deposited with the National Library of Ireland and kept under seal for fifty years. Described by Harriet Weaver as Joyce's 'staunchest and most loyal and devoted and understanding friend', Léon was murdered by Nazis the following year.

## – 84 –

In January 1941, Joyce took a walk down the familiar Bahnhofstrasse with his grandson. Twenty-five years earlier the same street had inspired a poem called 'Zurich 1918'. The final lines read:

Ah star of evil! star of pain!
Highhearted youth comes not again.

Nor old heart's wisdom yet to know
The signs that mock me as I go.

That night Joyce woke in the early hours with unbearable stomach pain. In the morning he was taken to the Red Cross Hospital where an X-ray revealed he was suffering from a duodenal ulcer that had remained untreated for years, leading to perforation. Immediate surgery was advised. Joyce initially refused to undergo the operation because it was too expensive. His last words to Giorgio were: 'But how are you going to pay for this?'

Following surgery, for a few days it seemed as though he was making a good recovery. Blood transfusions were given by two young men from Neufchatel, which Joyce saw as a good omen, joking that he liked Neufchatel wine.

While recuperating, Joyce asked for a makeshift bed for Nora to be placed next to his. The doctors resisted the suggestion and urged her to go home and rest. The patient was out of danger, she was assured.

That night, 13 January 1941, Joyce woke at 1am and asked for his wife, and then relapsed into a coma caused by peritonitis.

At 2.15am James Joyce died.

*Alone, a long, a last the*

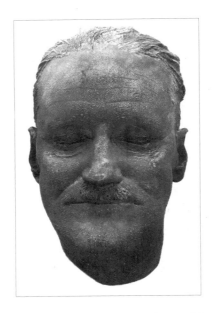

Death mask of James Joyce, located in the
James Joyce Tower and Museum

# CODA:

## *Nora*

Nora chose a funeral wreath in the shape of a harp. She commented to a friend:

> I chose this shape for my Jim who so loved music.

After burying her husband, Nora was left with an unemployed, divorced son who had inherited his father's drinking habits, a grandson whose mother was absent, and a daughter who was in a mental hospital many miles away. She was also left without money. A group of Joyce's friends passed around the hat, writing a letter to Joyce admirers in the United States appealing for contributions to go towards support of James Joyce's dependants:

> No sum would be too small. We have received many $1 bills sent by students.

Some of the items Paul Léon had rescued from the Paris apartment were sold in order to raise funds. Harriet Weaver again came to the rescue, sending Nora money even though she was aware that a good portion of it would be spent on cognac, Giorgio's preferred intoxicant.

Nora made enquiries about bringing her husband's body back to Dublin. She was bitterly disappointed when the Irish authorities showed no interest in Joyce's remains. Many assumed that Nora would want to return to live in Ireland. She responded:

> They burnt my husband's books. I will never go back.

Suffering from rheumatism and arthritis, Nora shuffled between cheap, poorly heated pensions while waiting for the settlement of Joyce's estate. She was so poor that she wrote to a friend:

> I am afraid I shall sooner or later have to sell my manuscript of Chamber Music written in Dublin in the year 1909 and dedicated to me; it is written on parchment and bound in cream coloured leather with the Joyce crest on one side of the cover and our initials on the other side. If you know anybody who you think will be interested in buying such a work would you kindly let me know.

Seven years after Joyce's death, despite Nora's straitened circumstances and severe arthritis, a visitor from Dublin observed:

> Even that has not affected her serenity, her impeccable poise, her almost regal appearance.

Nora would remain in Zurich for the rest of her life, eventually moving to a comfortable, centrally heated hotel-pension. In April 1951 she died in a convent hospital and was buried beside her husband.

Afterwards, her grandson commented:

> She was a rock. I venture to say that he could
> have done none of it, written not one of the
> books without her.

## Lucia

In 1951, Lucia was transferred from Ivry, France, to
St Andrew's Hospital, Northhampton, in England, at
Harriet Weaver's expense, who was now Lucia's legal
guardian. There she received irregular visitors, among
them Samuel Beckett. Lucia died in 1982 and was
buried in Northampton, according to her wishes. Her
medical records have not been released.

## Giorgio

Giorgio remained in Zurich and was his mother's
constant companion until he married a German eye
doctor and moved to West Germany, where he died at
the age of 71.

Three members of the Joyce family are buried
alongside each other in Fluntern Cemetery, Zurich.
The inscription of the family tombstone reads: 'James
Joyce, Nora Joyce, Giorgio Joyce', followed by a
blank for one more name.

## Harriet Shaw Weaver

Harriet Shaw Weaver became Joyce's literary
executrix. At Nora's insistence, the manuscripts of

*Finnegans Wake* were donated to the British Museum rather than the National Library of Ireland because she believed that Ireland had 'never appreciated' her husband. Weaver died in England in 1961.

## Sylvia Beach

Sylvia Beach remained in Paris during World War II and was interned for six months. She published a memoir of her time as a bookseller called *Shakespeare and Company* in 1959 and died in Paris two years later. The American bookseller George Whitman named his bookshop *Shakespeare and Company* in honour of Beach in 1964. Whitman's daughter, Sylvia Whitman, now runs the bookshop at 37 rue de la Bûcherie on the Left Bank.

## Stephen

Stephen spent the war in a boarding school in Switzerland and then, at the age of fourteen, decided he wanted to reunite with his mother in the United States, who had by then recovered from her mental illness. He graduated from Harvard University and worked with the OECD until resigning to attend full-time to his grandfather's literary estate, which he guarded zealously, regularly threatening legal action against biographers, scholars and artists wanting to quote from Joyce's books and correspondence. In 2004, in the lead-up to the centenary of *Ulysses*, Stephen threatened the Irish government with a lawsuit and as a result all public readings for Bloomsday were cancelled. On one occasion he threatened to sue a Joyce enthusiast who had memorised sections of *Finnegans Wake,* claiming that by doing so he had likely 'already infringed' on the estate's copyright. When Stephen Joyce died in 2020 the worldwide Joycean community breathed a sigh of relief.

### *Ulysses in Australia*

In 1941, the same year James Joyce died, *Ulysses* was banned in Australia for a second time. The Minister for Customs was quoted as saying:

> It's blasphemous, indecent and obscene and I say it cannot be tolerated any longer in Australia. Why a thing like this has been allowed into Australian homes for years is beyond me.

*Ulysses* would remain banned until 1954.